CITYSPOTS
VALENCIA

Jo Whittingham

Thomas Cook

D0718870

Written by Jo Whittingham
Updated by Renée van der Meulen

Published by Thomas Cook Publishing
A division of Thomas Cook Tour Operations Limited
Company registration No: 1450464 England
The Thomas Cook Business Park, 9 Coningsby Road
Peterborough PE3 8SB, United Kingdom
Email: books@thomascook.com, Tel: +44 (0)1733 416477
www.thomascookpublishing.com

Produced by The Content Works Ltd
Aston Court, Kingsmead Business Park, Frederick Place
High Wycombe, Bucks HP11 1LA
www.thecontentworks.com

Series design based on an original concept by Studio 183 Limited

ISBN: 978-1-84157-878-1

First edition © 2006 Thomas Cook Publishing
This second edition © 2008 Thomas Cook Publishing
Text © Thomas Cook Publishing
Maps © Thomas Cook Publishing/PCGraphics (UK) Limited
Transport map © Communicarta Limited

Series Editor: Kelly Anne Pipes
Production/DTP: Steven Collins

Printed and bound in Spain by GraphyCems

Cover photography (City of Arts and Sciences) © Ripani Massimo/4Corners Images

CONTENTS

SYMBOLS KEY

The following symbols are used throughout this book:

@ address ❶ telephone ❺ fax ⓦ website address ❺ email
🕒 opening times ⊘ public transport connections ❶ important

The following symbols are used on the maps:

🄸 information office		▦ points of interest	
✈ airport		◯ city	
✚ hospital		○ large town	
🛡 police station		◦ small town	
🚌 bus station		══ motorway	
🚆 railway station		▬ main road	
Ⓜ metro		minor road	
✝ cathedral		— railway	
❶ numbers denote featured cafés & restaurants			

Hotels and restaurants are graded by approximate price as follows:
£ budget price ££ mid-range price £££ expensive

Abbreviations used in addresses:
Av.   Avenida (Avenue)
C/   Calle (Street)
Pl.   Plaza (Square)

❶ *The Miguelete belfry towers over Plaza de la Reina in the Old City*

INTRODUCING
Valencia

Introduction

Radiant in the bright Mediterranean sunlight and fragrant with the scent of orange blossom, Spain's third-largest city seems curiously untouched by tourism when so much of the nearby coastline has disappeared under high-rise resorts. Valencia not only has immense charm, but also fantastic weather, engaging museums, fabulous shopping, perfect beaches, crazy fiestas and a population with a reputation for partying that is second to none. How many other cities can match that?

Valencia's rich history is laid out in the buildings of its beautiful Old City, with medieval churches, Renaissance trading halls and baroque mansions built over the remains of the Roman town. For centuries, the town nestled in a bend of the Turia River, but after catastrophic flooding in 1957, which caused terrible damage and loss of life, the river's course was diverted and in its place the city now has a wonderful park that stretches out for 14 km (9 miles) through its centre.

Valencia will really fluff your rice. Indeed, paella was first cooked in the orange groves that thrive in the city's reliably warm, sunny weather; where better to enjoy the dish than in a restaurant by the city's sandy Playa de la Malvarrosa (Malvarrosa Beach)? The Old City's thriving café culture and great restaurants are also a must, as is the Barrio del Carmen district's vibrant, sexy nightlife.

More than 30 museums allow visitors to explore every aspect of Valencian culture, from prehistoric settlers, to local crafts and products and, of course, the famous fiestas that bring normal city life to a halt each year. The population reserves all its energy for the most raucous of these, *Las Fallas*, which fills the Old City's squares with gargantuan *papier mâché* sculptures that are dramatically set ablaze as part of a climactic fireworks show.

Valencia is, right now, staking its claim to be a major European city, and breathtaking new developments such as the incredible Ciutat de les Arts i de les Ciències (City of Arts and Sciences) complex demonstrate a real sense of creativity and confidence. Why not come and see what you think?

▲ *Valencia's town hall*

When to go

Valencia is a top destination at any time: the good vibes are year-round and so is the friendly welcome. If you're particularly heat-averse, it's probably better to avoid the height of the summer, though there's no shortage of bars and cafés in which to take refuge. Costs don't vary on- and off-peak as much as in some cities, although in summer it is best to book everything – especially accommodation – well in advance.

SEASONS & CLIMATE

If it is true that the weather affects our mood, then the average 300 days of sunshine that enliven Valencia each year might go some way to explaining why it is such a happy and easy-going city. The mild Mediterranean climate ensures that even in winter the temperature rarely drops below 10°C (50°F), while in high summer it often nudges up to above 30°C (86°F). July and August are the hottest and sunniest months, but many people find this heat oppressive in the city and traditionally this is when the locals take their holidays. Although spring and autumn are when the most rain falls, usually as infrequent and refreshing light showers, the daytime temperatures hover pleasantly between 22°C (72°F) and 28°C (82°F). Even in the winter, however, it is often warm enough to wander around in your shorts.

ANNUAL EVENTS

There is always something going on in Valencia, whether it is one of the many traditional festivals (which often have a religious theme that's celebrated with a decidedly secular zeal) or one of the increasing number of sporting and cultural events that the city now attracts; Valencia's positive energy and the gregarious nature of its population

◆ *Each May, Our Lady of the Forsaken is carried through the city*

make it an ideal place in which to let the good times well and truly roll.

January

Parade of the Three Wise Men (5 January) Crowds gather to watch colourful floats pass by and enjoy the spectacle of the wise-guys being lifted onto the Town Hall balcony.

St Vincent the Martyr Procession (22 January) A joyous morning procession dedicated to the city's patron saint sets off from the cathedral and winds all over town. By lunch time, Valencia is one big party. ⦿ Metro: Angel Guimerá, Xátiva; bus: 4, 6, 8, 9, 11

March & April

Las Fallas (12–19 March) The biggest – and bangingest – festival of the year (see page 12).

Semana Santa Marinera (Sailors' Holy Week) (starts 17 March 2008; 5 April 2009) Sailors? Devout? Who knew? Well, the entire population, obviously, because everybody celebrates a marine thanksgiving by flocking to the Turia River Park for a riot of the sailors' favourite on-leave pursuits, picnicking and kite-flying.

May & June

Our Lady of the Forsaken (10 & 11 May 2008; 11 & 12 May 2009) This celebration kicks off with a spectacular Saturday night concert in Plaza de la Virgen, followed by fireworks and dancing in the Turia River Park. The Sunday morning sees crowds gather to watch the image of the Madonna carried shoulder-high from the basilica to the cathedral next door. Fireworks at 14.00 are followed by an evening procession when the image is carried through the Old City and showered with petals.

Feast of Corpus Christi (25 May 2008; 9 June 2009) This has been celebrated since 1355, and today the huge procession makes an unforgettable spectacle as it passes through the streets bringing biblical characters to life. Don't miss the bizarre figures of giants and Cabezudos – huge, beskirted figures with oddly exaggerated heads – that come first.

July

Batalla de Flores (Flower Battle) (23 July 2008; 24 July 2009) This traditional procession on the Avenue Alameda sees Carnival Queens, carried in beautifully adorned carriages, throwing thousands of petals at the crowds as they glide by.

August

European Grand Prix (22–24 August 2008; 23–25 August 2009)
The portside areas that were modernised and spruced up for the
America's Cup in 2007 now form the circuit for Formula 1's newest
street race. Ⓦ www.formulaunovalencia.com

October

Valencia Film Festival (3rd week in October) Less showy than Cannes,
less po-faced than London, this is one of the leading festivals in
a country where the seventh art is held in especially high regard.
Ⓦ www.mostravalencia.com

PUBLIC HOLIDAYS
Expect shops and services in Valencia to be partially
or entirely closed on these dates.
New Year's Day 1 Jan
San José 19 Mar
San Vicente Ferrer 5 Apr
Good Friday 21 Mar 2008; 10 Apr 2009
Easter Monday 24 Mar 2008; 13 Apr 2009
Labour Day 1 May
Assumption of Mary 15 Aug
Sant Dionís (Valencian Community National Day) 9 Oct
All Saints' Day 1 Nov
Day of the Constitution 6 Dec
Feast of the Immaculate Conception 8 Dec
Christmas Day 25 Dec

Las Fallas: flaming amazing

There can be few cities whose population spends all year raising money to finance the creation of enormous *papier mâché* sculptures, which artists labour over for months, in the knowledge – nay, expectation – that, one night in spring, they'll be set ablaze and reduced to dust in front of ecstatic crowds. Welcome to *Las Fallas*, Valencia's craziest week, when thousands of locals and thousands more tourists pour onto the streets to welcome the coming spring with deafening firecrackers, opulent parades and the burning of nearly 400 incredible, satirical creations in the squares.

The city's fondness for fiery festivity probably has its origins in the medieval carpenters' practice of burning the wooden stand that had held their oil lamp all winter when evenings began to get lighter in spring. These small desk fires have evolved into the fully fledged pyromania that underpins this popular fiesta today.

Valencia fills with revellers for *Las Fallas*, but if you do manage to get a room in the Old City between 12 and 19 March, then be prepared to be rudely awoken by the early morning *despertà*, a distressing combination of firecrackers and marching bands. But then you'll want to be up early so you have time to see the exhibition of the *ninots* (small, sculpted figures that caricature prominent Spanish and international celebrities, particularly from the world of politics), and the amazing flower-offering to Our Lady on the evenings of the 17th and 18th, when the immaculately dressed *Fallas* Queens (*Falleras*) parade to Plaza de la Virgen with baskets of flowers.

It's fascinating to watch the painstaking construction of the sculptures in the squares of the Old City during the night of 15 March; come midnight on the 19th, the festival's climax, they are all consumed by flames. Only one *ninot* is spared (as a result of a public vote), and placed in the Museo Fallero (Fallas Museum, see page 103).

Another must-witness are the *mascletas*, huge, cacophonous daytime fireworks shows that you can enjoy at 14.00 every day during the festival, in the Plaza del Ayuntamiento. The high point of the nocturnal fireworks displays is the spectacular and deafening *Nit de foc* (Night of Fire), which is usually on 18 March, at around 01.00.

That's the way to welcome in the spring – with a bang.

⬤ *The huge Fallas sculptures are destined to go up in smoke*

History

Roman Valentia was founded in 138 BC as a tranquil seaside resort in which distinguished military men could enjoy their retirement. Once the Romans were gone, however, the city's fortunes pitched turbulently between prosperity and disaster right up until the end of the 20th century.

Visigoths had control of the city in the 6th century AD, but by 709 Islamic Moors were in occupation, and under their influence Valencia became a booming centre of trade in paper, silk, leather and ceramics. Muslim rule continued, with a brief break when the city was captured by the infamous mercenary Rodrigo Díaz de Vivar (El Cid) in 1094, until it was conquered by the Christian King Jaime I of Aragón in 1238. Under his reign, Valencia became the wealthy capital of a new kingdom.

This marked the beginning of the city's most prosperous period, when important local institutions were established and the city grew beyond all recognition as people arrived hoping to share in

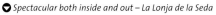
● *Spectacular both inside and out – La Lonja de la Seda*

the wealth of the thriving port. By the 16th century, Valencia had become one of the most important trading ports on the Mediterranean and contained many great buildings, including La Lonja de la Seda (Silk Exchange, see page 64).

However, by the end of that century complacency had set in among the ruling classes, which was spectacularly illustrated by the expulsion of the city's Moors (who by then had converted to Christianity) and Jews in 1609. This left local agriculture with hardly any labour and Valencia rapidly descended into economic collapse. Almost a century later, the city backed the losing Hapsburg side during the War of the Spanish Succession, which resulted in the loss of the region's autonomous status when Philip V of Spain seized power. Trade in silk facilitated economic recovery later in the 18th century, but successive wars continued to blight the city.

Worse was to come, however, when the city became the capital of the Spanish Republic during the Spanish Civil War (1936–9), after its government and courts were ousted from Madrid by General Francisco Franco's Nationalist rebellion. Valencia surrendered in March 1939, and, after three years of bloodshed, General Franco eventually succeeded in overthrowing the Republic and established a dictatorship that lasted until 1975.

Following the return of democracy, the region of Valencia was granted autonomous status in 1982 and local people were once again free to speak their own Valenciano language. Today's Valencia – the Valencia that's been modernised, equipped and marketed with sufficient aplomb to have seduced such demanding customers as the governing bodies of both the America's Cup and Formula 1 racing (in 2003 and 2007 respectively) – is, to a great extent, the realisation of the dreams and vision of one woman, Rita Barberá Nolla, who has been overwhelmingly returned as Mayor at every election since 1991.

Lifestyle

Spain is a nation that knows how to let its hair down and have a good time; but even other Spaniards revere Valencia as a party city. Its open and friendly population excels in the laid-back lifestyle that many stressed-out visitors initially find so foreign (but then part of the pleasure of a stay in the city is winding down to the local pace of life). Valencians are proud of their region's autonomous status and speak their own language, Valenciano, which is similar to Catalan. This can cause confusion when the local street names don't match those on maps printed in Spanish, but passers-by are always happy to help.

When they are not working (expect businesses, museums and galleries to close for a two-hour lunch break, between 14.00 and 16.00), Valencians love to spend time in street cafés or bars with friends or family, where loud, animated conversations are the only entertainment required. This social scene continues into the night, when families with children will stay out until late and the younger generation head out to bars and clubs until the early hours.

It is forbidden by Spanish law to smoke in workplaces, in public buildings and on public transport. In small bars and restaurants, it is up to the owner to decide whether or not to allow smoking (a sign reading *Se Permite Fumar* – smoking permitted – will be visible on the door). Those bars and restaurants that are bigger must have a set-aside smoking area. It is illegal to sell tobacco to under-18s. However, you may still find people smoking in those areas where it is forbidden.

The city all but shuts down in August, when the heat gets too much and the population goes on holiday. The majority of shops,

⬣ *Make like a local and take a break at a street café*

as well as bars and restaurants, close every Sunday because Valencia remains devoutly Roman Catholic. It is considerate to dress and behave in an appropriate manner when visiting churches, because worshippers inside may easily be disturbed or offended.

Culture

Many people might think that Spain's Mediterranean coast consists of sun, sand, sangria and little else, but the city of Valencia is out to set the record straight. Its long and colourful history, with its healthy infusions of different races and religions, has left a fascinating cultural legacy which modern Valencia is striving to preserve and build upon.

More than 30 museums around the city lay every aspect of Valencian life and culture bare for the visitor to explore. Archaeological evidence has shown that even when the Romans arrived, people had already been living in the area for thousands of years. The Centro Arqueológico de la Almoina (Archaeological Centre of the Almoina, see page 71), located in the heart of the city, has exhibits from historical periods going way back. For centuries this region has manufactured beautiful ceramics, and the wonderful Museo Nacional de Cerámica, aka 'Gonzalez Martí', (Gonzales Martí National Ceramics Museum, see page 73) demonstrates how this craft developed through the ages, while also providing glimpses of life in the baroque palace where the museum is housed. Mementos of the city's favourite fiesta, *Las Fallas* (see page 12), can be found in the Fallas Museum (see page 103).

Art is not neglected here either, in fact the IVAM Centre Julio González (Valencian Institute of Modern Art–IVAM, see page 72) was Spain's first modern art gallery when it opened in 1989. It has been so successful that it has already outgrown its original building and 2005 saw work begin on a project to add a larger perforated 'skin' to the site to expand the exhibition space. The Museo de Bellas Artes

⬤ *You couldn't describe the exterior of the Ceramics Museum as understated*

(Museum of Fine Arts, see page 103) would also benefit from more space to display its awe-inspiring collections that stretch from glistening, golden, 13th-century religious art to the sensitive depiction of local life by 19th-century artists. The bodies of work by artists from the city in both museums are impressive and leave you feeling that you know the city a good deal better once you have seen them.

There is plenty of highbrow entertainment on offer here, too, particularly since many of the fabulous traditional theatres have been restored to their former glory. Although the majority of theatre productions will not be accessible to those who do not speak Spanish or Valenciano, there are numerous jazz, dance and opera performances here. In fact the latest addition to Valencia's cultural repertoire was opened late in 2005; the opera house, grandly known as the Palau de les Arts Reina Sofía (see page 103), is an incredible state-of-the-art building designed by the local architect Santiago Calatrava as part of La Ciutat de les Arts i de les Ciències (the City of Arts and Sciences complex). It clearly signals Valencia's intention to make its mark on the cultural map and add to the treasures that it already holds.

▶ *Valencia reveals a feast of architectural styles, from medieval to modern*

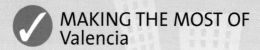
MAKING THE MOST OF
Valencia

Shopping

It comes as a surprise to many first-time visitors, but Valencia is a great place to shop. A compact network of shopping streets fills the southeast corner of the Old City between Calle Paz and Calle Colón, making it easy to navigate the huge selection of designer boutiques and high-street names on foot (but do watch out for the traffic).

Spanish fashion designers such as Adolfo Domínguez have a strong presence in the city, as do the more accessible fashion chains like Mango (see page 79) and Zara (see page 81). While designer goods are only marginally cheaper here than in the UK, there is a marked difference in the price of the high-street brands, many of which are almost half the UK price, so it might be worth only half-filling your suitcase.

Valencia is a centre of shoe manufacture and there are some amazing shoe shops, selling huge ranges of leather footwear at reasonable prices. A cluster that should keep you going for an hour or so can be found on Calle Don Juan de Austria.

Ceramics have also been a local speciality for centuries, with many traditional cafés and bars still decorated with the once-ubiquitous elaborately painted tiles. A few such tiles can be picked up for a modest price at the Sunday market in Plaza Redonda (see page 77), along with hand-painted fans, leather goods and books.

On a Sunday morning, apart from visiting the quaint, round Redonda market, it is also worth heading out to the Mestalla Flea Market (see page 105), next to the football stadium. This giant gathering of stalls in a car park is a great place to hunt for a bargain and marvel at the quirky items on sale. The best market of all

USEFUL SHOPPING PHRASES

What time do the shops open/close?
¿A qué hora abren/cierran las tiendas?
¿A kay ora abren/theeyerran las teeyendas?

How much is this?
¿Cuánto es?
¿Cwanto es?

Can I try this on?
¿Puedo probarme esto?
¿Pwedo probarme esto?

My size is ...
Mi número es el ...
Mee noomero es el ...

I'll take this one, thank you
Me llevo éste
Meh llievo esteh

This is too large/too small/too expensive.
Do you have any others?
Es muy grande/muy pequeño/muy caro. ¿Tienen más?
Es mooy grandeh/mooy pekenio/mooy karo. ¿Teeyenen mas?

however, Mercado Central (see page 77), is open every day except Sunday and is a gigantic food market with almost 1,000 stalls, in a beautiful, completely restored *modernista* (art nouveau) building. This is probably the loveliest place in Valencia in which to suffer an understandably massive shopaholic relapse.

Eating & drinking

Eating and drinking here, as in most of Spain, is a real pleasure due to the abundance of fresh produce and the genuine love that the people have for preparing and consuming their treasured local dishes. The only difficulty for tourists may be adjusting to Valencian meal times: a typical breakfast of bread, ham and cheese eaten around 10.00 needs to power you through until lunch, which sometimes is not served in restaurants until 14.00. This afternoon meal is usually a leisurely affair, especially on hot, sunny days, while dinner in the evening is never eaten much before 21.00 and goes on until 23.00.

Valencia is the true home of paella, which was originally a modest meal made over a wood fire by workers in the orange groves. The rice constituent was (and still is) grown around the Albufera lake (see page 118). Today, city restaurants serve numerous variations of this dish, with seafood, beans and meat, but many assert that genuine Valencian paella should contain rabbit and chicken.

A slightly more unusual local delicacy worth trying is *all i pebre*, a favourite in the wetlands around the Albufera lake, where men still fish for eels – in this dish they are stewed in a garlic and red pepper sauce. If you take a trip to El Palmar, south of the city, stop off at a restaurant to sample this speciality.

PRICE CATEGORIES

The restaurant price guides used in this book indicate the approximate cost of a three-course meal for one person, excluding drinks.

£ up to €25   ££ €25–40   £££ over €40

One of Spain's most famous sweets, eaten especially during the Christmas holiday season, *turrón*, also hails from the Valencia region. The delicious confection is made from almonds, egg white

🔺 *Valencia is the home of paella*

and honey, sometimes in a hard form known as *Alicante* and sometimes as a soft nougat called *Jijona*.

Horchata (*'orxata'*) is a mysterious form of liquid refreshment on sale in cafés and *horchaterias* around the city. Residents swear by their 'tiger nut milk' to cool off on a hot day, and the opaque mixture of crushed *chufa* nuts, cinnamon, sugar and water, sipped through a straw and accompanied by *fartons*, sticks of sweet soft bread, is delicious and certainly worth trying. A more familiar drink is the juice from Valencia's famous oranges, which tastes utterly superior to anything that comes out of a carton and is often served as a dessert in restaurants. If you see what look like large pitchers of orange juice being served in bars they are likely to be the potent *Agua de Valencia*; a delicious, if extremely alcoholic, combination of orange juice, cava and vodka.

There are many excellent restaurants in the city to choose from, but if you are looking for a cheap light lunch or quick snack try a tapas bar (often, the smaller and plainer the better). Throughout the day you can order a drink with anything from a dish of olives to a spread of small plates of meat, fish or potato dishes, ideal for sharing. This is a great chance to try something new, so do venture beyond *patatas bravas* (fried potatoes with a spicy sauce).

It pays to be aware that, in many tapas bars, the further you sit from the bar itself, the more you will be charged for your food. Something similar is also true in many restaurants with street terraces, where you may be charged extra for sitting outside. If you look at the menu closely, any extra charges should be made clear, as should whether the stated prices include IVA tax (the Spanish

● *The balmy summer evenings are perfect for dining outdoors*

version of VAT), which is charged at 7 per cent. The service charge however, is always included in your bill, so any tip is at your discretion; 5 per cent is considered ample.

If a picnic lunch is more up your *avenida*, then make a beeline for the Mercado Central (see pages 77), where you can buy all kinds of delicacies in the bustling surroundings of one of the largest local markets in Europe. A good second-best are the basement supermarkets in the El Corte Inglés department stores (see page 78) that are scattered liberally around the city and have bakeries, delicatessens, fresh produce and plenty of other temptations. Once you have your supplies, go to one of the cool, shady parks, such as the Turia River

● *The Mercado Central is a great place to buy fresh food*

Park (see page 100) or the Jardines de Real Viveros (Royal Gardens, see page 94), or head to the city's Playa de la Malvarrosa (Malvarrosa Beach, see page 99), whose fine sand is likely to add some crunch to your lunch.

USEFUL DINING PHRASES

I would like a table for ... people
Quisiera una mesa para ... personas
Keyseeyera oona mesa para ... personas

May I have the bill, please?
¿Podría traerme la cuenta por favor?
¿Pordreea trayerme la cwenta por fabor?

Waiter/waitress!
¡Camarero/Camarera!
¡Kamarero/Kamarera!

Could I have it well-cooked/medium/rare, please?
¿Por favor, la carne bien cocida/al punto/roja?
¿Porr fabor, la kahrne beeyen kotheeda/al poontoh/roha?

I am a vegetarian. Does this contain meat?
¿Soy vegetariano. ¿Tiene carne este plato?
Soy begetahreeahnoh. ¿Teeyene karneh esteh plahtoh?

Where is the toilet (restroom) please?
¿Dónde están los servicios, por favor?
¿Donde estan los serbeetheeos, por fabor?

Entertainment & nightlife

Valencia is known as a party city – you can expect to find vibrant nightlife, with locals, students and tourists packing the bars and clubs. The city's club culture is tremendously varied, ranging from small, dark indie dives, to intense Latin and salsa venues and some of the glitziest – and ritziest – haunts around. If you are planning to spend an evening at one of the more glamorous spots, dress to impress, because the bouncers are well known for their pickiness; and don't even think of turning up before midnight.

The majority of visitors, along with many locals, will spend their nights out in the Old City, where there is a concentration of bustling bars and clubs around Calle Caballeros, in the Barrio del Carmen district. Here there are quirky bars with atmospheric terraces set out in the old squares and always another place to try down the next alleyway.

Summer is the season to head down to the bars by the beach, which seem to stay open even later than those in the centre. Several noisy places nestle among the restaurants on the promenade, but there are also some trendy bars and clubs on Calle Eugenia Viñes, a street that's set back from the beach. The students tend to congregate in the lively bars around Avenida Blasco Ibáñez and Avenida Aragón, out towards the university, which are still within easy reach of the Old City. Meanwhile a slightly older, professional crowd drinks in the more expensive bars near Plaza Cánovas del Castillo and gets dressed-up for nights in the flashy clubs on Gran Vía Germanías at the weekend.

If live music is more your thing, then it's easy to find good jazz and local indie and rock bands playing small venues almost every night of the week. There are local listings magazines and websites that will help you find out exactly who is playing during your visit. Of course there are also the two major classical music venues in the Turia River Park, at the Palau de la Música (the concert hall, see page 104) and Palau de les Arts Reina Sofía (the opera house, see page 103), which between them have an extensive programme of concerts, opera and dance. The city's theatres are highly thought of and host productions throughout the year, except August. Bear in mind that plays are performed in either Spanish or Valenciano.

Despite the obvious fact that most of the blockbuster films shown in the city are dubbed into Spanish, there are several smaller cinemas that show films in their original language (see page 114). If you check up-to-date listings there is usually a film screening in English somewhere, and it will cost about half as much to see it as it would in a UK cinema. **UGC CineCité** (❸ Av. Tirso de Molina 16 ❶ 963 17 35 90 ⓦ www. ugc.es ⓜ Metro: Turia; bus: 95) in the Mercado Fuencarral Valencia shopping centre shows films in English (look out for VOS – *versión original subtitulada*, 'original version with subtitles').

Each venue has its own box office, but if you need to book ahead, most tickets can be reserved and paid for via the tourist information office's *Turis Valencia* website (ⓦ www.turisvalencia.es).

Also available free in tourist information agencies, bars, restaurants and hotels is *24–7* magazine (ⓦ www.24-7valencia.com), which has features and listings covering bars, clubs and local entertainment in English. *Valencia City* (ⓦ www.valenciacity.es) is another urban magazine offering interviews about culture and music, listings of bars, clubs, hotels and all the latest local entertainment. It's on sale for one euro in newsagents and tourist information centres.

Sport & relaxation

SPECTATOR SPORTS

As host city for one of the Spanish legs of the Formula 1 Grand Prix, Valencia knows all about staging events that attract thousands of spectators.

Consistently riding high in Spain's top football league, Valencia CF are the city's heroes. The **Mestalla Stadium** (ⓐ Av. de Suecia ① 963 37 26 26 ⓦ www.valenciacf.es ⓜ Metro: Aragón; bus: 32), close to the city centre, is packed for Saturday night matches, and if you can get a ticket it makes for supreme entertainment. These highly prized items are available from the stadium box office two to three days before a match.

For those fans who would like to go home with the official T-shirt or other memorabilia, there is the official **Valencia CF Shop** (ⓐ C/Pintor Sorolla 25 ① 963 51 47 42 ⓦ www.valenciacf.es ① 10.00–21.00 Mon–Sat, closed Sun ⓜ Metro: Colón; bus: 70, 71, 81), opposite the Corte Inglés in the city centre.

Controversial, but still incredibly popular in the city itself, bullfighting takes place in the grand **Plaza de Toros** (ⓦ plazadetorosdevalencia.com) during the March and July seasons. Tickets are available from Museo Taurino (Bullfighting Museum, see page 100).

PARTICIPATION SPORTS

Valencia's prime position on the Mediterranean coast makes it a haven for water sports, including sailing, scuba-diving and kite surfing. Three great organisations to investigate are:

Brisas de Valencia Boat This is a rental company with a programme of excursions. ⓐ Offices: C/Puebla de Valverde 6 ① 963 69 31 89

Ⓦ www.brisasdevalencia.com Ⓛ 11.00–13.00, 17.00–20.00 Mon–Fri, closed Sat & Sun Ⓜ Metro: Hospital; bus: 70

Centro de Buceo Bentos An outfit that runs accredited diving courses for all levels. Ⓐ C/Pavía 31 Ⓣ 963 56 45 05 Ⓦ www.infonegocio.com/bentos Ⓜ Metro: Les Arenes; bus: 20, 21, 22, 23, 32

Kite Surf Oliva You can learn to kite surf from April to September just south of Valencia. Ⓐ Playa de Rabdells (near Hotel Oliva Nova Golf), Oliva Ⓣ 637 10 21 00 Ⓦ www.kitesurfoliva.com

Golf enthusiasts will enjoy playing the region's courses in Valencia's excellent climate. Try:
Club de Golf Escorpión A well-kept 27-hole private course located in the Camp de Turia area. Ⓐ Carretera S. Antonio Benagéber-Bétera, Km 3 Bétera Ⓣ 961 60 12 11 Ⓦ www.clubescorpion.com Ⓘ Tourists only Mon–Fri; a reservation is required

Golf El Saler One of Spain's top courses. Ⓐ Parador El Saler, Av. de los Pinares 151 Ⓣ 961 61 03 84 Ⓦ www.parador.es Ⓘ Please book in advance as the course is not open to the general public during tournaments

RELAXATION
Balnearia For the ultimate in relaxation, try one of this city spa's luxurious chocolate-and-wine treatments. Ⓐ Av. Aragón 29 Ⓣ 963 69 32 32 Ⓦ www.spabalnearia.com Ⓛ 10.00–22.00 Mon–Sat & holidays, closed Sun Ⓜ Metro: Aragón; bus: 10, 12, 41, 79

Accommodation

The phenomenal number of luxury hotels built on the beach and the streets leading to the port after Valencia got the green light for the America's Cup means that visitors now have many amazing locations to choose from. Prices rise when demand is high, so if you want to stay when there's a big event in town, brace yourself to pay through the nose and make sure you book as far in advance as possible. Spring and autumn are great times to visit the city and if you shop around you can find excellent rates.

Although tourists often choose to stay in the historic city centre, there's no need to rule out the rest of the city, and for sun worshippers there are great hotels right on the beach. If you are particularly sensitive to noise pollution, remember that the bars and clubs in the Barrio del Carmen area stay open until the early hours, and you might find a hotel there a touch thin-walled.

Spain has a baffling range of accommodation classifications. *Paradores* are state-owned, luxury hotels that can be good value, but are never cheap; hotels have a good range of facilities and comfortable rooms; *hostales* (not the same as hostels) are small, cheaper hotels with limited facilities; *pensions* are a useful budget option and provide a simple room for the night; *fondas* will be similar to pensions, but with dining facilities. The official star

PRICE CATEGORIES

The ratings below indicate the approximate cost of a room with en-suite facilities for two people for one night.

£ up to €65   ££ €65–100   £££ over €100

system is based on the facilities provided rather than charm
or quality of service.

HOTELS

Ibis Valencia Palacio de Congresos £–££ Located near Valencia's
large congress venue, this good, basic hotel is well connected to
the Old City by public transport. ⓐ C/Valle de Ayora ⓣ 963 17 33 37
ⓦ www.ibishotel.com ⓔ H3314@accor.com ⓝ Metro: Empalme;
tram: Palau de Congresos; bus: 62, 63

🔺 *One of the beautiful rooms of La Casa Azul – La Ruta de la Seda (The Silk Route)*

Hotel Continental ££ Close to the Plaza Ayuntamiento and the Old City sights, this slightly dated hotel has large, homely rooms and good facilities. ❸ C/Correos 8 ❶ 963 53 52 82 Ⓦ www.contitel.es Ⓜ Metro: Xátiva; bus: 10

Valencia ££ Ideally located close to the train station, this good-value hotel has modern, ensuite rooms, with TV and air-conditioning. ❸ C/Convento San Francisco 7 ❶ 963 51 74 60 Ⓦ www.hotel-valencia.com Ⓜ Metro: Xátiva; bus: 7, 5B

Ad Hoc Monumental ££–£££ A cosy and friendly favourite; the rustic decoration emphasises the beautiful vaulted ceilings and exposed brickwork of this restored 19th-century house in the Old City. ❸ Boix 4 ❶ 963 919 140 Ⓦ www.adhochoteles.com Ⓜ Metro: Angel Guimerá, Xátiva; bus: 7, 5B, 27, 28, 60

La Casa Azul £££ A city-centre hotel housed in a beautiful, 19th-century building. There are only three rooms, but each of them is a little gem. The furniture comes from local antique shops and is for sale (as is the art on the walls). ❸ C/Palafox 7 ❶ 963 51 11 00 Ⓦ www.lacasaazulvinosandrooms.com Ⓜ Metro: Angel Guimerá, Xátiva; bus: 7, 5B, 27, 28, 60

Hilton £££ Located opposite Valencia's congress hall, this 29-floor hotel is the biggest in the city. As it's also the loftiest, its designer rooms have panoramic views. ❸ Av. Cortes Valencianas 52 ❶ 963 03 00 00 Ⓦ www.hilton.com Ⓜ Metro: Empalme; tram: Palau de Congresos; bus: 62, 63

Hotel Balinero Las Arenas £££ A beachfront development that's more Miami than Valencia, with opulent rooms and great facilities, including an Olympic-size pool. ❸ C/Eugenia Viñes 22–24 ❶ 963 12 06 00 Ⓦ www.hotel-lasarenas.com Ⓝ Tram: Les Arenes; bus: 32, 21

Hotel Jardín Botanico £££ A small, boutique hotel, with contemporary décor and rooms boasting whirlpool baths and king-size beds. ❸ C/Doctor Peset Cervera 6 ❶ 963 15 40 12 ❸ info-reservas@hoteljardinbotanico.com Ⓝ Metro: Angel Guimerà, Turia; bus: 81, 60, 7

Hotel Sorolla Palace £££ An architectural gem, this hotel offers everything you'd expect from a 5-star billet. ❸ Av. Cortes Valencianas 58 ❶ 961 86 87 00 Ⓦ www.hotelsorollapalace.com Ⓝ Metro: Empalme; tram: Palau de Congresos; bus: 62, 63

Neptuno £££ Right on the beach, this chic boutique hotel has high-spec rooms with plasma TVs and massage baths. ❸ Paseo de Neptuno 2 ❶ 963 56 77 77 Ⓦ www.hotelneptunovalencia.com Ⓝ Metro: Neptú; bus: 20, 22, 23

Palau de la Mar £££ A palatial building in the Old City, immaculately converted into a luxurious hotel with exquisite bathrooms and an excellent restaurant. The Spa & Wellness centre is a real must. ❸ Av. Navarro Reverter 14 ❶ 963 16 28 84 Ⓦ www.fuenso.com ❸ hospes.palaudelamar@hospes.es Ⓝ Metro: Colón; bus: 2, 4, 10, 71, N8

HOSTALES

Hostal Antigua Morellana £ Charming place in the centre of town, in a renovated 18th-century building. Very clean, with friendly hosts. C/En Bou 2 963 57 73 www.hostalam.com Metro: Angel Guimerá, Xátiva; bus: 7, 5B, 27, 28, 60

Miramar ££ Basic but modern rooms all with a bathroom, TV, air-conditioning or fan and a fabulous location right on the beach. Paseo de Neptuno 32 963 71 51 42 www.petitmiramar.com Metro: Neptú; bus: 19, 32

YOUTH & BACKPACKER HOSTELS

Hilux Valencia – Feetup Hostels £ Comfortable rooms with balconies, works of art by local artists, and in the city centre, too. C/Cadirers 11 -1° 963 91 46 91 hilux@feetuphostels.com Metro: Turia, Angel Guimerá; bus: 5B

Hôme Youth Hostel £ A friendly place for budget travellers. Clean, basic rooms, no curfew and great location in the Old City. C/La Lonja 4 963 91 62 29 www.likeathome.net Metro: Angel Guimerá, Xátiva; bus: 7, 5B, 27, 28, 60

CAMPSITE

Devesa Gardens £ Almost a holiday resort on its own, with swimming pools, a mini-zoo and a huge range of activities, as well as pitches for tents and caravans and top-notch facilities. Carretera El Saler (13 km south of Valencia) 961 61 11 36 www.devesagardens.com Bus: Devesa Gardens

Boutique-style hotels, like the Palau de la Mar, offer a modern touch

THE BEST OF VALENCIA

For a flavour of Valencian life from the Middle Ages to the modern day, spend time in the Old City. Here you'll find the cathedral, many churches, amazing historic buildings, magnificent squares full of street cafés, some of the finest museums and galleries, as well as the greatest concentration of restaurants and most vibrant nightlife. Of course there is plenty to see outside the Old City too, and if you plan to do a whistle-stop tour of the sights and museums in just a few days, buy a Valencia Card (see page 54).

TOP 10 ATTRACTIONS

- *Las Fallas* Valencia's week-long March fiesta climaxes with the burning of gigantic satirical sculptures (see page 12)

- **La Ciutat de les Arts i de les Ciències (City of Arts and Sciences)** An inspired collection of modern public buildings (see page 90)

- **La Lonja de la Seda** Mesmerising spiral columns stretch to the vaulted ceiling of this incredibly beautiful Renaissance Silk Exchange, a UNESCO World Heritage Site (see page 64)

🔻 *The cloisters at the Real Colegio del Patriarca are an unmissable sight*

- **Catedral & Miguelete** This building contains important artworks and the Holy Chalice. Climb the bell tower for panoramic views (see page 60)

- **Mercado Central** Delicious local produce sold in a beautifully restored, glorious art nouveau building (see page 65)

- **Paella** Eat the traditional rabbit and chicken variety in its city of origin (see page 24)

- **Playa de la Malvarrosa (Malvarrosa Beach)** If you can't take the city heat, take the tram to the beach (see page 99)

- **Real Colegio del Patriarca (Royal College of the Patriach)** Valencia's most beautiful church (see page 68)

- **Museo de Bellas Artes (Museum of Fine Arts)** A fascinating collection of art spanning the 13th–19th centuries (see page 103)

- **Museo Nacional de Cerámica 'Gonzalez Martí' (Gonzalez Martí National Ceramics Museum)** An opulent baroque palace displaying the city's finest ceramics (see page 73)

Suggested itineraries

HALF-DAY: VALENCIA IN A HURRY

If time is short, begin in the Old City with a visit to the cathedral
and a dash to the top of the Miguelete bell tower (see page 63)
for the magnificent view. Pause for refreshment with a glass of
horchata and *fartons* in a café on Plaza de la Virgen, then visit
the late-Gothic Lonja de la Seda (Silk Exchange, see page 64) and
the bustling Mercado Central (see page 65). As a contrast, walk
through the park in the old Turia riverbed (see page 100) to see the
striking, white structures of the Ciutat de les Arts i de les Ciències
(City of Arts and Sciences, see page 90) and treat yourself to dinner
in the Submarino restaurant (see page 111).

1 DAY: TIME TO SEE A LITTLE MORE

A few extra hours will give you time to visit one of the attractions
at the City of Arts and Sciences, and there might be time to
squeeze in some evening shopping. Head to Calle Don Juan de
Austria (see page 74) for chain-store bargains, and Calle Sorní
(see page 105) for designer names.

2–3 DAYS: TIME TO SEE MUCH MORE

Make the most of a longer stay to delve deeper into the city's
culture and spend time in museums and galleries; the Museo de
Bellas Artes (Museum of Fine Arts, see page 103) is a good place to
start. Embrace the Mediterranean habit of long, laid-back lunches
and lingering late-night meals, followed by nights out in the
Old City's vibrant Barrio del Carmen, sipping a cheeky
Agua de Valencia.

LONGER: ENJOYING VALENCIA TO THE FULL

It's easy to get used to Valencia's relaxed pace of life and warm, sunny weather, so test your adaptability by spending a day at the Playa de la Malvarrosa (Malvarrosa Beach, see page 99), and enjoy a delicious paella for lunch at one of the promenade restaurants. You could even head out of the city to the dune-backed beach at El Saler (see page 123) or the tranquil Albufera lake (see page 118) and surrounding nature reserves.

◑ *Even if you have little time, make sure you see the City of Arts and Sciences*

Something for nothing

When the holiday euros are running low, Valencia still has plenty to offer. Although the admission charge for most museums is no more than €2 anyway, many admit visitors gratis on Saturday afternoons and all day Sundays. The Museo de Bellas Artes (Museum of Fine Arts,

⬤ *A walk in Turia River Park – once occupied by a river – is free*

see page 103) has free admission and enough amazing works of art to occupy most visitors for hours.

For an experience that's literally and figuratively priceless, visit the domed church of the Old City's Real Colegio del Patriarca (see page 68) at 09.30. Every day (except Monday) at this time there is Gregorian chanting, which creates a solemn, magical atmosphere.

The fab weather means that venturing into the great outdoors is a real pleasure. There is an incredible amount of green space close to the city centre, including the park that fills the full 14 km (9 mile) length of the old Turia riverbed, which is perfect for walking, relaxing and picnicking (see page 100). The soft, golden sand of the Malvarossa Beach (see page 99) is also only a short tram ride from the city centre and is great for a day's swimming, sunbathing, castle building or kite flying. For a zero-euro investment that will pay enormous dividends straight into your feel-good exchequer, spend a few hours wandering in the Jardín Botánico (Botanic Gardens, see page 93) and benefit shamelessly from the expertise and industry of the city's finest horticulturalists. The greenhouse there really is chill city central, and it's as free as sunshine... as indeed is the sunshine that will almost certainly grace your entire visit and give you some of the most beautiful sunrises and sunsets you'll ever see.

If your visit coincides with one of the many fiestas, then there will probably be more free entertainment than you can handle. The week of 12–19 March, for example, is devoted to *Las Fallas* (see page 12). Putting in an appearance at the tomato bombardment that is *La Tomatina* (see page 133) in the little town of Buñol will transport you joyously back to your childhood and present you with all the free purée you could ever wish to smell. Many other spectacular – and free – processions snake through the streets of the Old City to mark important dates in the Catholic calendar.

When it rains

The rain in Spain may not be confined exclusively to the plain but it certainly doesn't reach Valencia very often. On average, the city has 300 days of sunshine each year and any rainfall tends to be in short, sharp showers rather than day-long downpours, so it is unlikely to spoil any of your holiday plans. It is more likely that you will want to spend some time indoors to get out of the heat and sun than the wet, but whatever your motivation, Valencia has plenty of indoor activities to enjoy.

In a city with more than 30 museums and art galleries, there is bound to be something for everyone. The impressive IVAM Centre Julio González (Valencian Institute of Modern Art, see page 72) has a popular photographic collection, alongside permanent exhibitions of the work of local artists Pinazo and González, while the Museo Fallero (Fallas Museum, see page 103) is full of weird and wonderful *ninots* (small sculptures) from the *Fallas* festivals.

A trip to the Ciutat de les Arts i de les Ciències (City of Arts and Sciences, see page 90) will not disappoint. Children will love the 'touch everything' policy in the Museu de les Ciències Príncipe Felipe (Prince Phillip Science Museum, see page 96), and the hi-tech cinema, planetarium and laserium shows that are projected onto the central dome of L'Hemisfèric (see page 93) make great entertainment. In the amazing aquarium complex of L'Oceanogràfic (see page 96), you can lose yourself for hours, watching sharks and stingers glide effortlessly past.

Why not head for the shopping streets between Calle Paz and Calle Colón (see page 74) for some retail therapy? There are enough designer boutiques, high-street stores and fabulous shoe shops to distract you for hours, so any rain is likely to have stopped long before you emerge from your retail reverie. First-rate pampering is available at the city's beauty spas. Balnearia (see page 33) offers a huge range of beauty and relaxation treatments, including chocolate therapies and an indulgent wine bath. On second thoughts, perhaps it doesn't rain often enough.

🔺 *L'Oceanogràfic offers shelter if it rains, and a chance to learn*

On arrival

TIME DIFFERENCE
Spain follows Central European Time (CET). During Daylight Saving Time (late Mar–late Sept), the clocks are put ahead one hour.

ARRIVING
By air
In order to accommodate the huge increase in passenger numbers over recent years, Aeropuerto de Valencia (Valencia Airport) at Manises has been expanded with a new terminal (handling both arrivals and departures), including a metro line that links it directly to the city just 8 km (5 miles) away. There are cafés, a restaurant, shops and ATMs, plus a tourist information office in arrivals where you will find maps and advice on where to stay.

Aeropuerto de Valencia ⓐ Carretera del Aeropuerto ① 961 598 500 ⓦ www.aena.es

---

◐ *Estación del Norte by night*

Taxis to the city centre will cost between €14 and €17, depending on the time of day and your exact destination. The taxi rank is opposite the exit from arrivals, but you can call one of the following firms:

Radio Taxi Manises ❶ 961 52 11 55

Radio Taxi Valencia ❶ 963 70 33 33

The Aerobus shuttle service takes you directly into Valencia. There are stops on three of the city's main streets: Avenida del Cid, Calle Bailén and Calle Angel Guimerá. The bus runs every 20 minutes between 06.00–22.00 and costs €2.50.

Metro lines 3 and 5 take you into the centre of the city in about 30 minutes, and the journey will cost €1.70.

By rail

The Estación del Norte, on Calle Xátiva, is Valencia's main RENFE station. This beautiful *modernista* (art nouveau) building is one of the city's architectural gems. There are restaurants, shops, chemists, ATMs and a tourist information office. Step out of the station and you are on the southern edge of the historic city centre and close to the Xàtiva metro station if you need to travel further afield.

Estación del Norte ❸ C/Xátiva 24 ❶ 902 24 02 02 ❿ www.renfe.es
Ⓜ Metro: Xátiva; bus: 5, 19, 35

By road

If you are driving into Valencia from the north or south, then the roads signposted from the A-7 motorway will bring you into the centre of the city. After that, however, navigating and parking in the Old City are both tricky and the roads can get extremely busy. Much of the rest of the city is laid out on a grid pattern, where the long, wide thoroughfares make finding your way easier. There are plenty of public car parks and you'll see big indicators along the main roads with information as to which is the closest and whether there are free spaces or not. Local drivers can be unforgiving and impatient with hesitant visitors behind the wheel. Stick to public transport unless you have nerves of steel and an up-to-date road map.

Just north of the historic city centre, on Avenida Menéndez Pidal, is the city's bus station. This is where both national and international buses arrive. There are places to eat and it is next to the **Nuevo Centro Shopping Centre** (ⓐ Av. Pio XII 5 ⓦ www.nuevocentro.es). Taxis are available, just outside the station's main exit.

Estación Central de Autobuses ⓐ Av. Menéndez Pidal 11 ⓣ 963 46 62 66 ⓜ Metro: Turia; bus: 8, 78, 80

FINDING YOUR FEET

Valencia is a busy, bustling city, but the pace of life is incredibly relaxed (locals love to joke about their *mañana* attitude). People are friendly, happy to help tourists and can often speak English. Valencia is a religious city, so try to be respectful when visiting churches by dressing appropriately and considering whether a camera flash will disturb people. It is also a relatively safe city with a low crime rate, although it makes sense to keep bags and cameras secure in busy areas and on the beach. Few of the streets, even the tiny ones in the Old City, are closed to traffic, so keep your wits about you and remember that trams run along some roads, too.

ORIENTATION

While you are unlikely to get completely lost in the Old City centre, its maze of winding streets and alleyways, hemmed in by tall buildings, means that to start with at least you won't always know exactly where you are. The fact that many street names are in Valenciano does not help, although common sense is usually enough to match

IF YOU GET LOST, TRY ...

Excuse me, do you speak English?
Perdone, ¿habla usted inglés?
Perdoeneh, ¿ahbla oosteth eengles?

**Excuse me, is this the right way to the Old City/the city centre/
the tourist office/the station/the bus station?**
Perdone, ¿por aquí se va al casco antiguo/al centro de la ciudad/a la
oficina de turismo/a la estación de tren/a la estación de autobús?
*Perdoneh, ¿por akee seh bah al kasko antigwo/al thentroe de la
theeoodath/al offeetheena deh toorismoe/a la estatheeon de
trenes/a la estatheeon dey awtoebooses?*

Can you point to it on my map?
¿Puede señalármelo en el mapa?
¿Pwede senyarlarmelo en el mapa?

them up. The Old City is bounded by the Turia River Park (see page 100)
to the north and a semicircle of large boulevards to the south, along
the line of the city wall, neither of which you will pass without noticing.

The Old City's squares are the best places to head for if you get lost.
Plaza de la Reina, just south of the cathedral, has one of the six tourist
information offices in the city (see page 149), and Calle Paz, one of
the main shopping streets, leads off it. A good way to avoid getting
lost outside the Old City is to head through the Turia River Park.

The maps in this book show the main sights, but many of the
restaurants, clubs and shops that are listed are on smaller streets.

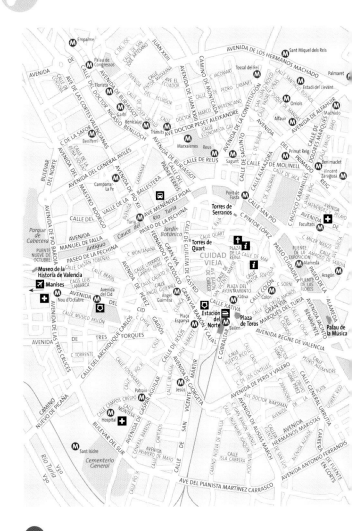

If you are planning to stay for longer than a couple of days, it's a good idea to acquire a detailed map of the city from a local news-stand or bookshop or from the tourist information office.

GETTING AROUND

The public transport system is great. The four metro lines (L1, L3, L5, L6) and one tramline (T4) run from 05.30–24.00 daily, while the buses run until 22.30 Mon–Fri, with reduced services on Sundays and holidays.

The metro is cheap and easy to use; the stations have small, circular, red signs with a white 'm'. Single metro tickets are €1.30 and can be bought from ticket offices or machines in stations. A Bono Bus is valid for 10 trips on the bus and costs €5.65. A T1 ticket is a one-day pass for the metro, trams and buses and costs €3.30. A T2, for two days, costs €5.65 and a T3, for three days, costs €8.25. A Bono Transbordo is a 10-trip pass for all three and costs €7. These combined tickets are also available from tobacconists and kiosks. The **Valencia Card**, available from tourist information offices, hotels, tobacconists and kiosks, is valid for 1–3 days (€7–15) and allows unlimited travel on the metro, trams and buses, as well as other reductions and discounts in museums, restaurants and shops. For more information about the Valencia Card visit ⓦ www.valenciatouristcard.com or call ☎ 900 70 18 18.

Buses are run by EMT and every stop has clear timetable and route information. Single tickets are €1.20 and can be bought from the driver. Night buses run from 23.00–03.00, depending on the line. Bus lines 20–23 only run in summer.

The city's licensed taxis have a green light on their roof and are for hire when this is illuminated. The numbers next to this light indicate which tariff is being operated, depending on the time of day. A trip from the Old City to the beach will cost €5–7. Normally taxi drivers in Valencia are friendly, but if you do have any stress, contact

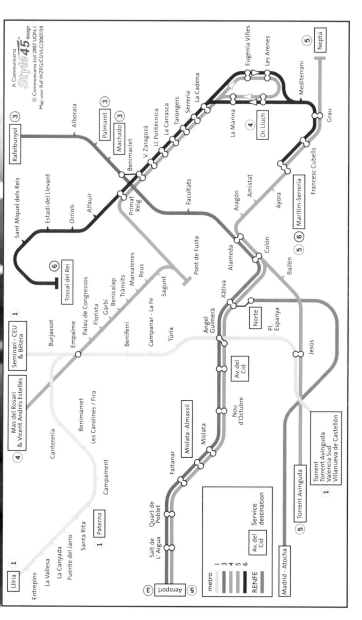

the **Metropolitan Transport Authority** (ETM ☎ 963 16 07 07).

If you plan to head out of the city, regional trains leave from Estación del Norte (see page 93). Some lines also leave from Estación de Cabañal on Avenida Blasco Ibáñez. Regional buses usually leave from the Estación Central de Autobuses (see page 50) and may stop elsewhere on their route through the city.

Metro ☎ 900 46 10 46 Ⓦ www.metrovalencia.com
EMT buses ☎ 963 15 85 15 Ⓦ www.emtvalencia.es

CAR HIRE

It is only really worth hiring a car if you plan to leave the city and explore the surrounding area. There are plenty of rental companies at the airport and close to Estación del Norte that should supply you with a compact vehicle for around €40 per day, although pre-booking via your airline's affiliates should secure you reductions.

Avis

🅐 Estación del Norte, C/Xátiva 24 ☎ 963 52 52 00 🅕 963 52 24 78
Ⓦ www.avis.es 🕐 08.00–22.00 Mon–Sat, 10.00–21.00 Sun
Ⓜ Metro: Xátiva; bus: 5, 19, 35
🅐 Aeropuerto Manises ☎ 961 52 21 62 🅕 961 52 21 62 Ⓦ www.avis.es
🕐 07.00–23.59 Mon–Sat, 08.00–23.59 Sun Ⓜ Metro: Aeroport

Europcar

🅐 Estación del Norte, C/Xátiva 24 ☎ 963 51 90 55 Ⓦ www.europcar.es
🕐 08.00–22.00 Mon–Sat, 10.00–21.00 Sun Ⓜ Metro: Xátiva; bus: 5, 19, 35
🅐 Aeropuerto Manises ☎ 961 52 18 72 🅕 961 59 86 94
Ⓦ www.europcar.es 🕐 07:00–23.59 Ⓜ Metro: Aeroport

⏺ *The Porta de la Mar leads to the Turia River Park*

THE CITY OF
Valencia

The Old City

At Valencia's heart is its Old City; a romantic labyrinth of ancient, cobbled streets winding among grand houses and opening out onto magnificent squares. Tourists and locals alike flock here to visit the city's most famous sights and wander among the fascinating mix of Gothic, Renaissance, baroque and *modernista* (art nouveau) buildings that makes Valencia unique. The crowds are not only drawn here by the architecture, but also by the vibrant street cafés, which line the elegant Plaza de la Virgen and Plaza de la Reina close to the cathedral and fill many of the smaller squares that are tucked away, off nearby streets. These places serve coffee, alcohol and often the local *horchata* (tiger nut juice), as well as excellent tapas and make great vantage points for people-watching.

The compact nature of the Old City means it is easiest to explore on foot and, although it is tricky to navigate, you will never stray far without stumbling upon an easily recognised building – those ornate belfries and substantial fortified towers are excellent landmarks – or the encircling Turia River Park (see page 100) to the north and large, bustling boulevards to the south. Once you have had your fill of the sights, make for Calle Paz, Calle Colón and the streets in between, to spend some time in Valencia's excellent shops, which open well into the evening.

There's no need to leave this area as the sun sets, because it has some of the best restaurants and liveliest nightlife. The district known as Barrio del Carmen (between Calle Caballeros and the Turia River Park) is the place to go at night.

One way of ensuring that you don't miss a thing is to take a guided tour. **Valencia Guias** (ⓐ Paseo de la Pechina 32 ⓣ 963 85 17 40 ⓦ www.valenciaguias.com, www.valenciabikes.com

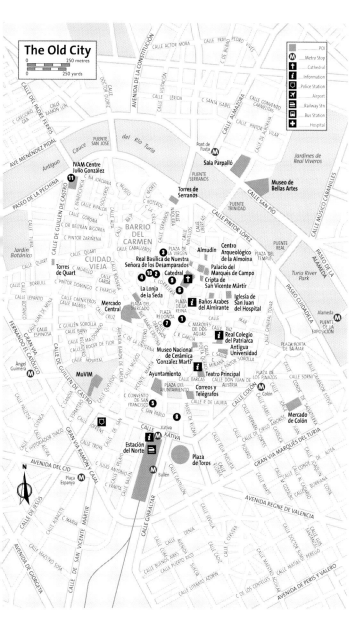

🅜 Metro: Turia; bus: 95 ❶ Charge for tour) run an excellent two-hour walking tour of the Old City's key sights from the main door of the tourist information office at the Plaza de la Reina (see page 150), every Saturday at 10.00. Just meet the guide there or book through your hotel.

SIGHTS & ATTRACTIONS

Baños Árabes del Almirante (Islamic Baths)

Step back in time to when the Moors ruled the city, with a visit to the beautiful Islamic baths. Built in the 12th or early 13th century, this building has been restored to show its original layout and design. Wonderful, star-shaped skylights illuminate many of the rooms. ❷ C/Baños del Almirante 3 ❶ 605 27 57 84 ❹ 10.00–14.00, 18.00–20.00 Tues–Sat, 10.00–14.00 Sun, closed Mon 🅜 Metro: Angel Guimerá, Xátiva; bus: 4, 6, 8, 9, 11

Catedral & Tribunal de las Aguas (Cathedral & Water Tribunal)

Constructed between 1262 and 1426, Valencia's cathedral has been well used and added to ever since. Its three main doors provide a quick lesson in the city's key architectural styles; the earliest is the Romanesque *Puerta del Palau*, which opens onto Calle del Palau, next to the Archbishop's Palace; next came the Gothic *Puerta de los Apóstoles*, with its finely wrought representations of the 12 apostles; finally, in the early 18th century, the baroque *Puerta de los Hierros* was added next to the bell tower.

Along the length of the interior are private chapels, one of which was paid for by the renowned local Borgia family and contains two

❶ *Catedral Valencia*

⬥ The centre of Valencia – Plaza del Ayuntamiento

paintings by Goya. Other relics include the dessicated arm of St Vincent the Martyr and the Holy Chalice, a red agate cup, which, according to local legend, was used by Jesus at the Last Supper. It is also worthwhile climbing the 262 steps to the top of the 50-m-tall (165 ft) Gothic bell tower, known as the Miguelete, for a panoramic view of the city.

Every Thursday, the *Tribunal de las Aguas* (Water Tribunal) convenes in the cathedral doorway to settle farmers' water-related disputes; there aren't many these days, but it would be a shame to stop a thousand-year-old custom.

Part of the cathedral is always open to those wishing to attend masses, but the remaining part, including the museum, can only be visited using a multilingual audio-guide tour. ⓐ Pl. de la Reina ❶ 963 91 28 27 ⓦ www.catedraldevalencia.es ⓛ 10.00–18.30 Mon–Sat, 14.00–18.30 Sun & holidays, 20 Mar–31 Oct; 10.00–17.30 Mon–Sat, closed Sun & holidays between 14.00–17.00, 1 Nov–19 Mar ⓝ Metro: Angel Guimerá, Xátiva; bus: 4, 6, 8, 9, 11. Admission charge

Cripta de San Vicente Mártir (Crypt of St Vincent the Martyr)
Archaeological excavations in this 13th-century chapel, dedicated to the martyred St Vincent, unearthed the remains of a Visigoth chapel, which can be seen today, along with interesting displays of artefacts that demonstrate how this site has developed through the ages. A fascinating audiovisual show explores the building's colourful past. ⓐ Pl. del Arzobispo 2 ❶ 963 94 14 17 ⓛ 09.30–14.00, 17.30–20.00 Tues–Sat, 09.30–14.00 Sun, closed Mon ⓝ Metro: Angel Guimerá, Xátiva; bus: 4, 6, 8, 9, 11. Admission charge; entry tickets available at the Palacio del Marqués de Campo (City Museum, see page 73).

Iglesia de San Juan del Hospital (Church of San Juan del Hospital)

Valencia's oldest church was founded in 1238, after Christians recaptured the city from the Moors; in fact two 13th-century crusaders' crosses can still be seen painted by the entrance. The original Romanesque and Gothic features of the church were masked by a 17th-century baroque interior, but this was badly damaged when the church was looted and burned during the Civil War in 1936 and finally removed when restoration began in 1966. This was the year that the diocese gave the church to the priests of Opus Dei, a controversial wing of the Catholic Church. ⊙ C/Trinquete de Caballeros 5 ❶ 963 92 29 65 ⓦ www.sanjuandelhospital.es ⓛ 07.00–08.00, 09.30–13.30 & 17.00–21.30 Mon–Fri, 09.30–13.30, 17.00–21.30 Sat, 11.00–14.00, 17.00–21.30 Sun & public holidays ⓜ Metro: Colón

La Lonja de la Seda (Silk Exchange)

This magnificent Gothic building was constructed as a trading hall for silk merchants in the 15th century, when Valencia was Spain's most prosperous city, and today is listed as a UNESCO World Heritage Site. Inside the hall, towering columns, resembling bales of silk, spiral up from the original marble floor to support the vaulted ceiling and create the most beautiful space. Careful inspection of the decorative carvings inside and out reveals some unexpectedly mischievous scenes – a reminder that this was a civil building that did not restrict the masons to religious subjects. There is also a patio filled with orange trees, a tower for imprisoning dishonest merchants and a Renaissance wing, which was home to the city's first modern bank. ⊙ Pl. del Mercado ❶ 963 52 54 78 ext. 4153 ⓛ 10.00–14.00, 16.30–20.30 Tues–Sat, 10.00–15.00 Sun, closed Mon ⓜ Metro: Angel Guimerá, Xátiva; bus: 7, 5B, 27, 28, 60

▲ *The Silk Exchange is on the list of UNESCO World Heritage Sites*

Mercado Central (Central Market)

This beautifully tiled and domed *modernista* building opposite
La Lonja de la Seda contains one of Europe's largest markets.
Mouth-watering fish, vegetables, fruit, spices and cured meats
abound on the nearly 1,000 stalls. You can also find all sorts of
souvenirs, and even real paella pans in all sizes in the little shops
just outside, opposite the Lonja (Silk Exchange). ❷ Pl. de Mercado

🕿 963 82 91 00 🌐 www.mercadocentralvalencia.es 🕐 07.30–14.30 Mon–Sat, closed Sun Ⓜ Metro: Angel Guimerá, Xátiva; bus: 7, 5B, 27, 28, 60

Plaza del Ayuntamiento

Two important municipal buildings stand proudly in this wide, but curiously wonky, square. The **Correos y Telégrafos (Main Post Office)** was opened in 1923 and is magnificently topped with a sculpted metal, purely decorative, communications tower. Even if you have no real business to go inside, do peep in and look up at the beautiful glass-in-lead elliptic dome, showing the coats of arms representing the provinces of Spain (Ⓐ Pl. del Ayuntamiento 24 🕿 902 19 71 97 🕿 963 10 27 84 🌐 www.correos.es 🕐 08.30–20.30 Mon–Fri,

● You can stock up on every foodstuff at the huge Mercado Central

09.30–14.00 Sat, closed Sun ⓝ Metro: Xàtiva; bus: 32, 35). Opposite, the eclectic **Ayuntamiento (Town Hall)** is an 18th-century building with a 1920s façade . If you look inside you will find the elegant marble staircase, the glass hall and a beautiful council chamber (ⓐ Pl. del Ayuntamiento 1 ⓣ 963 52 54 78 (010 Town Hall general information) ⓦ www.valencia.es ⓛ 09.00–13.30 Mon–Fri (unless official business is underway) ⓝ Metro: Xàtiva; bus: 32, 35). Don't miss the **Museo Histórico Municipal (Municipal History Museum)**, which is housed in this building, showing emblematic pieces of the city, such as the Senyera (the Valencian flag), the sword of King James the Conqueror, maps, engravings and images (ⓣ 963 52 54 78).

Plaza de la Virgen

This marble-paved square, with its central fountain and street cafés, is a magnet for locals and tourists alike, not only because it is a great place to watch the world go by, but also because it is dominated by two of the city's most important churches: the Catedral (see page 60) and the Real Basílica de Nuestra Señora de los Desamparados.

Real Basílica de Nuestra Señora de los Desamparados (Basilica of Our Lady of the Forsaken)

This unusual 17th-century baroque church is packed for Sunday Mass, and its radiant, gem-encrusted, Gothic image of the Virgin is Valencia's most venerated shrine. Its dome is decorated with an immaculately restored fresco, which is the reason that no candles are lit, to prevent their soot blackening the masterpiece once again.

ⓐ Pl. de la Virgen ① 963 91 86 11 ⊕ 07.00–14.00, 16.00–21.00
Ⓜ Metro: Angel Guimerá, Xátiva; bus: 4, 6, 8, 9, 11

Real Colegio del Patriarca (Royal College of the Patriarch)

The school and seminary of the Patriarca complex were founded in 1583 by St Juan de Ribera, opposite the university so that it was convenient for students to attend classes. Today, tourists may visit the museum, which has an incredible collection of 16th- and 17th-century art, including works by Juan de Juanes and El Greco. The jewels in the complex's crown are the beautiful Renaissance cloisters, reckoned to be among Spain's best, and the spectacular church. Miraculously, the church avoided being set ablaze like so many others during the Spanish Civil War and the original frescoes seen through a haze of incense are breathtaking, as is Ribalta's depiction of the *Last Supper* above the altar. The best time to visit is at 09.30, when Gregorian chanting adds to the place's magical atmosphere (except on Mondays). Guided tours around the whole complex with its collection of artworks and library can be arranged.

Church ❸ off Pl. Colegio del Patriaca ❶ 07.30–11.30, 19.00–20.00
El Patriarca complex ❸ C/Nave 1 ❶ 963 51 41 76 ❶ 11.00–13.30
❽ Metro: Colon; bus: 26, 31. Admission charge

Torres de Serranos & Torres de Quart (Serranos & Quart Towers)

The only survivors from the demolition of the medieval city wall in the 19th century, these heavily fortified gateways still dominate their surroundings and are truly emblematic of Valencia. The moated Torres de Serranos was built in 1392 and has been restored so it

⬤ *More towers – the Torres de Serranos guarded the medieval city walls*

is safe to climb up to the battlements and enjoy the spectacular view along the old Turia River and across the historic city centre. The 15th-century Torres de Quart is an impressive sight, with its numerous cannon-ball craters from Napoleon's attack on the city. From the 17th century till the beginning of the 20th century these towers were a prison. Now they are restored and open to the public.

Torres de Serranos ❸ Pl. de los Fueros ❶ 963 91 90 70 ⏱ 10.00–14.00, 16.30–20.30 Tues–Sat, 10.00–15.00 Sun & public holidays, closed Mon Ⓣ Tram: Pont de Fusta; bus: 5, 5B, 6, 8, 11. Admission charge, except Sun & public holidays

THE VERY IDEA OF IT!

MuVIM (Museo Valenciano de la Ilustración y de la Modernidad –Valencian Museum of Enlightenment and Modernity) pursues a strange concept, being, as it is, dedicated to the history of ideas. The permanent *Adventure of Thought* display takes you on a journey through time and shows how ideas have developed from the Middle Ages up to the present day. The guided tour includes a visit to a monastery, where you can observe monks thinking about talking and talking about thinking. Temporary exhibitions dwell upon such themes as the various means of communication by which concepts are transmitted. ❸ C/Quevedo 10 ❶ 963 88 37 30 ⓦ www.muvim.es ⏱ 10.00–14.00, 16.00–20.00 Tues–Sat, 10.00–14.00 Sun & public holidays, closed Mon Ⓜ Metro: Angel Guimerá; bus: 60, 62, 70, 72 ❶ Don't forget to book in advance as tours are for groups of 20 people only

Torres de Quart ◎ Guillem de Castro 89/Pl. de Santa Ursula
🛈 963 52 524 78 🕑 10.00–14.00, 16.30–20.30 Tues–Sat, 10.00–15.00
Sun & public holidays, closed Mon Ⓜ Metro: Angel Guimerá;
bus: 5, 70, 60, 81

CULTURE

Valencia is fiercely proud of its culture and traditions and there are
so many museums dedicated to every aspect of life in the region
that it would take weeks to visit them all.

Almudín
Originally a 15th-century warehouse for the storage of wheat, this
interesting and attractive building is now a museum space that
houses temporary exhibitions and art installations. The impressive
central nave has a high wooden roof, and three of its walls bear
17th-century paintings. The lofty archways separating the lateral
naves give the room a welcoming, open feel. ◎ Pl. de San Luis
Beltrán 1 🛈 963 52 54 78 ext. 4521 🕑 10.00–14.00, 16.30–20.30
Tues–Sat, 10.00–15.00 Sun & public holidays, closed Mon
Ⓜ Metro: Colón; bus: 8, 11, 16, 26, 28. Admission free on Sun
& public holidays

Centro Arqueológico de la Almoina
(Archaeological Centre of the Almoina)
At the entrance of this museum, opened in the summer of 2007,
a huge screen welcomes the visitor with an audiovisual documentary
about Valencia's history. The real tour of the museum starts at the
lower level, which is where excavations unearthed the ruins that
can now be seen here. Other audiovisual shows recreate the thermal

baths and historical episodes such as the cholera epidemic.
Bronze models allow the visitor to visualise Valencia as it used
to be. ⓐ C/Baños del Almirante 3 & 5 ☎ 963 52 54 78 ext. 4173
🕒 16.00–20.00 Fri, 10.00–20.00 Sat & Sun, closed Mon–Thur
Ⓜ Metro: Angel Guimerá, Xátiva; bus: 4, 6, 8, 9, 11

IVAM Centre Julio González (Valencian Institute of Modern Art)

This was Spain's first modern art gallery. Works by local artists Julio
González and Ignacio Pinazo form two of the permanent collections,

🔽 *The Ceramics Museum includes the recreation of a traditional kitchen*

while the third is an impressive array of international photography. There are also temporary exhibitions that change regularly. A gift shop, a bookshop, a café and restaurant also share the building and are open to museum-goers and the passing public. 🄰 C/Guillem de Castro 118 🄸 963 86 30 00 🄦 www.ivam.es 🄻 10.00–20.00 Tues–Sun, closed Mon 🄼 Metro: Turia; bus: 5, 95. Admission charge, except Sun

Museo Nacional de Cerámica 'Gonzalez Martí' (Gonzales Martí National Ceramics Museum)

Constructed during the 15th century, the Palacio del Marqués de Dos Aguas, in which the museum is housed, was given a complete revamp in 1740 and became the astonishing, marble-clad, wedding cake of a baroque building that it is today. The well-preserved alabaster surround of the main door is truly exceptional. Even if you don't have the slightest interest in ceramics it is worth going inside to see the equally extravagant interior. 🄰 C/Poeta Querol 2 🄸 963 51 63 92 🄦 mnceramica.mcu.es 🄻 10.00–14.00, 16.00–20.00 Tues–Sat, 10.00–14.00 Sun & public holidays, closed Mon 🄼 Metro: Colón; bus: 26, 31. Admission charge, except Sat afternoon & Sun

Palacio del Marqués de Campo (City Museum)

Valencia's municipal art archives are displayed here and consist largely of paintings by local artists since the 15th century. There is also a surprisingly interesting exhibition of weights and measures used by the city's prosperous merchants and also sculptures and drawings by Ricardo Boix. The building itself is an attractive old aristocratic palace, typical of the city's manorial architecture. 🄰 Pl. del Arzobispo 3 🄸 963 52 54 78 ext. 4126 🄻 10.00–14.00, 16.30–20.30 Tues–Sat, 10.00–15.00 Sun, closed Mon 🄼 Metro: Colón; bus: 8, 11, 16, 26, 28

Teatro Principal

The city's oldest and most magnificent theatre, dating back to the 19th century, seats an audience of 830. This stage is usually home to spectacular productions in Spanish or Valenciano, but the programme of dance, jazz and opera should be more accessible for those whose language skills are lacking.
ⓐ C/Barcas 15 ❶ 963 53 92 00 ⓦ www.turisvalencia.es for tickets ⓦ Metro: Colón; bus: 4, 6, 8, 10, 16

RETAIL THERAPY

Valencia is serious about its shopping, and seems, conveniently, to have arranged itself into distinct shopping locales. Calle Paz, on the outskirts of the 'Golden Mile' (the area around the Palacio del Marqués de dos Aguas), is one of the city's most beautiful streets and is lined with jewellers and designer names. The streets between Calle Paz and Calle Colón have everything from exclusive boutiques to Spanish high-street giants. If you can fight your way through the crowds and lanes of traffic, there are some fabulous shops on Calle Colón. Traffic's not a consideration on the pedestrianised Calle Don Juan de Austria, which also has all the high-street stores, including the El Corte Inglés chain (see page 78). Calle Derechos, being more of an alley than a street, is comparatively quiet and has some fabulously funky boutiques.

Adolfo Domínguez Elegant, but affordable, this Spanish designer has two stores on Calle Colón. ⓐ C/Colón 52 & 72 ❶ 963 94 48 31 ⓦ adolfo-dominguez.com ⓛ 10.30–20.45 Mon–Sat, closed Sun ⓦ Metro: Colón; bus: 5, 10, 13, 32, 81

🔺 *Valencia is a designer shopping mecca*

Armand Basi Wearable, tongue-in-cheek fashion from this Spanish designer's shop is within a reasonable price range. Just about.
🔲 C/Colón 52 ☎ 963 514 806 🌐 www.armandbasi.com
🕐 10.30–14.30, 16.30–20.30 Mon–Sat, closed Sun
Ⓜ Metro: Colón; bus: 5, 10, 13, 32, 81

Boss Store Men One of the many Hugo Boss shops in Valencia, this is the only one offering the Selection, Black, Orange and Green collections. 🔲 C/Paz 14 ☎ 963 52 67 16 🌐 www.hugoboss.com
🕐 10.00–21.00 Mon–Sat, closed Sun Ⓜ Metro: Colón; bus: 4, 6, 8, 9, 11

Bugalú Fantastic, colourful clothes for men and women: extremely cool. ⓐ C/Derechos 22 ⓣ 963 91 84 49 ⓛ 10.00–14.00, 17.00–20.30 Mon–Sat, closed Sun ⓜ Metro: Angel Guimerá; bus: 4, 6, 7, 9, 11

Cactus Stylish clothes and jewellery for women, skilfully displayed in a tiny shop. ⓐ C/Derechos 35 ⓣ 963 91 53 70 ⓛ 11.00–14.00, 17.30–21.00 Mon–Fri, closed Sat & Sun ⓜ Metro: Angel Guimerá; bus: 4, 6, 7, 9, 11

Carolina Herrera A fabulously chic shop displaying stylish fashions and accessories for men and women from the needle of this well-known Venezuelan designer. ⓐ C/Paz 5 ⓣ 963 15 31 64 ⓦ www.carolinaherrera.com ⓛ 10.00–14.00, 16.30–20.30 Mon–Fri, 10.00–14.00, 17.00–20.30 Sat, closed Sun ⓜ Metro: Colón; bus: 4, 6, 8, 9, 11

ⓓ *Plaza Redonda offers late-night souvenir shopping*

MARKETS & SOUVENIRS

Mercado Central (Central Market) What has to be the city's most colourful shopping experience has hundreds of stalls overflowing with vegetables, fruit, meat, fish and even household goods. It's a great place to shop for a picnic or stock up with supplies of delicious ham or olive oil before you leave (🄰 Pl. de Mercado ☏ 963 82 91 00 🖝 www.mercadocentralvalencia.es 🕒 07.30–14.30 Mon–Sat, closed Sun 🄼 Metro: Angel Guimerá, Xátiva; bus: 7, 5B, 27, 28, 60).

Plaza Redonda is a quaint, circular market place with a central fountain, just a couple of streets from Plaza de la Reina, although there is also an entrance from Calle San Vicente Martir, via C/Pescadería. Its Sunday morning market is good for picking up cheap local ceramics and fans, though the sale of live birds may put some visitors off.

Corte Inglés Spain's number-one department store is on Valencia's main shopping streets and in most shopping centres, but this one has a great supermarket in the basement. ⓐ C/Colón 27 ❶ 963 15 95 00 Ⓦ www.elcorteingles.es ⏰ 10.00–22.00 Mon–Sat, closed Sun Ⓜ Metro: Colón; bus: 5, 10, 13, 32, 81

Loewe Classic, luxurious collections for men and women from this Madrid-based design house. Men's ⓐ C/Poeta Querol 7 ❶ 963 53 38 92 Ⓦ www.loewe.es ⏰ 09.30–14.00, 16.30–20.00 Mon–Sat, closed Sun Ⓜ Metro: Colón; bus: 26, 31. Women's ⓐ C/Marques de Dos Aguas 7 ❶ 963 53 38 90 ⏰ 09.30–14.00, 16.30–20.00 Mon–Sat, closed Sun Ⓜ Metro: Colón; bus: 26, 31

▲ *Upmarket Calle Paz offers both traditional and designer shops*

Mango This shop caries fast-moving fashions at appreciably cheap, Spanish prices. 🄴 C/Don Juan de Austria 7 🄾 963 51 37 07
🄦 www.mango.com 🄻 10.00–21.00 Mon–Sat, closed Sun
🄽 Metro: Colón; bus: 5, 10, 13, 32, 81

Massimo Dutti Beautiful collections at affordable prices. This is the only one of the many Massimo Dutti shops in Valencia that also offers childrenswear. 🄴 C/Colón 33 🄾 963 42 77 01
🄦 www.massimodutti.com 🄻 10.00–21.00 Mon–Sat, closed Sun
🄽 Metro: Colón; bus: 5, 10, 13, 32, 81

United Colors of Benetton At this shop, Benetton offers all three collections (men, women and children) at probably more economical prices than you'll find at home. ⓐ C/Don Juan de Austria 28 ⓣ 963 51 44 04 ⓦ www.benetton.com ⓛ 10.00–21.00 Mon–Sat, closed Sun ⓜ Metro: Colón; bus: 5, 10, 13, 32, 81

Women'Secret A vibrant selection of lingerie and swimwear: the perfect place to buy a bikini and hit the beach with a thong in your heart. ⓐ C/Don Juan de Austria 22 ⓣ 905 45 95 45 ⓦ www.womensecret.com ⓛ 10.00–21.00 Mon–Sat, closed Sun ⓜ Metro: Colón; bus: 5, 10, 13, 32, 81

Yak & Yeti Cluttered with reasonably priced ethnic jewellery, throws and ornaments, this is more Asia than Spain, and is fun to browse. ⓐ C/Paz 9 ⓣ 963 91 52 92 ⓕ 963 91 52 67 ⓛ 10.00–13.00, 16.30–20.00 Mon– Fri, 10.00–14.00, 17.00–20.30 Sat, closed Sun ⓜ Metro: Colón; bus: 4, 6, 8, 9, 11

Zak Kolel A little boutique with trendy, slightly hippy, fashion from independent Spanish designers. ⓐ C/Derechos 32 ⓣ 963 92 21 59 ⓛ 11.00–14.00, 17.00–20.30 Mon–Sat, closed Sun ⓜ Metro: Angel Guimerá; bus: 4, 6, 7, 9, 11

Zara Another familiar brand that's probably cheaper in Spain. ⓐ C/Don Juan de Austria 32 ⓣ 963 51 55 92 ⓦ www.zara.es ⓛ 10.00–21.00 Mon–Sat, closed Sun ⓜ Metro: Colón; bus: 5, 10, 13, 32, 81

◐ *Valencia's Old City is just the place for shopping and snacking*

TAKING A BREAK

Exhausted after excessive sightseeing and shopping? Well, the Old City is the best place to do as the Valencians do and sit down in a street café or restaurant for a long, lazy lunch break. There are also plenty of tapas bars, cafés and even *horchaterias* to try.

Bertal £ ❶ This place offers a great variety of foods, from yoghurt and ice creams of all tastes and colours, to pizzas and fresh fruit juice. ❷ Pl. de la Reina 12 ☎ 963 92 31 38 ● 07.00–22.00 Ⓜ Metro: Angel Guimerá; bus: 4, 6, 7, 9, 11

Bodeguilla del Gato £ ❷ A traditional tapas bar, with marble-topped tables and a street terrace. ❷ C/Catalans 10 (off Calle Caballeros) ☎ 963 91 82 35 ● 20.00–01.30 Tues–Sun, closed Mon Ⓜ Metro: Angel Guimerá; bus: 4, 6, 7, 9, 11

Caféteria la Virgen £ ❸ Sit out on the terrace and enjoy coffee, beer and light lunches. ❷ Pl. de la Virgen 3 ☎ 963 91 70 72 ● 08.00–01.00 Ⓜ Metro: Angel Guimerá; bus: 4, 6, 7, 9, 11

The Lounge £ ❹ Friendly, Irish-owned bar with a selection of good-value salads, pitta bread sandwiches and Spanish-influenced dishes. ❷ C/Estamiñeria Vieja 2 (off Calle Correjería) ☎ 963 91 80 94 Ⓦ www.theloungecafébar.com ● 16.00–01.30 Ⓜ Metro: Plaza España, Xátiva; bus: 7, 5B, 27, 28, 60

Sandwichtown £ ❺ Unsurprisingly, a sandwich bar that also serves funky salads and baguettes. ❷ C/Convento San Francisco 3 ☎ 963 81 30 40 Ⓦ www.sandwichtown.es ● 08.00–19.00 Mon–Fri, 08.00–01.30 Sat, closed Sun Ⓜ Metro: Xátiva; bus: 6, 8, 10, 11, 35

● *A favoured establishment if you want to try a cooling drink of* horchata

Valor Chocolaterías £ ❻ For a real energy boost, try the intensely rich hot chocolate here. This is also the best place on the square for coffee and cake. ❷ Pl. de la Reina 20 ❶ 963 15 21 98 ❸ 08.30–22.00 Mon–Thur, 09.00–01.00 Fri, 09.00–02.00 Sat, 09.00–22.00 Sun ❽ Metro: Angel Guimerá; bus: 4, 6, 7, 9, 11

AFTER DARK

The Old City is where everyone in Valencia comes to party. At the weekends tourists and locals spill out of the trendy clubs and bars onto relaxed street terraces, enjoying the good-time atmosphere until well into the early hours. For the best nightspots and some of the most fashionable restaurants, head to the Barrio del Carmen district, north of Calle Caballeros, and take your pick.

Valencia has its share of chic, modern restaurants as well as tapas bars

RESTAURANTS

El Kiosko £ ❼ A traditional *cervecería* (beer bar), where you can take a seat for a drink or incredibly cheap (and fabulously tasty) tapas. ❸ C/Derechos 38 ❶ 963 91 59 82 ❶ 07.30–24.00 ❶ Metro: Plaza España; bus: 7, 27, 28, 81

Lizarrán £ ❽ For those wanting to experience the real thing, the tapas and *montaditos* (slices of French bread with the most delicious toppings) are a must. ❸ Convento Santa Clara 9 (off Paseo de Ruzafa) ❶ 963 51 40 30 ❶ 08.00–24.00 Mon–Fri, 11.00–24.00 Sat & Sun ❶ Metro: Xátiva; bus: 10, 17, 19

MaraMao Gran Caffé Italiano £ ❾ Creative Italian cuisine served in a dimmed-light atmosphere, with jazz and lots of candles. Try the Italian wines. ❸ C/Corregería 37 ❶ 963 92 31 74 ❶ www.valencia-in.com/maramao ❶ 14.00–17.00, 20.00–24.00 ❶ Metro: Angel Guimerá; bus: 4, 6, 7, 9, 11

El Rall ££ ❿ This tiny place specialises in the region's rice dishes and also serves fine fish and meat. The terrace is a real draw on warm evenings. ❸ C/Tunidores 2 (near La Lonja) ❶ 963 92 20 90 ❶ 13.30–15.30, 20.00–23.30 ❶ Metro: Plaza España; bus: 7, 27, 28, 81

La Sucursal £££ ⓫ Try the sample (*degustación*) menu and let the chef choose the meal for you, but make your own selection from the extensive wine list. ❸ C/Guillem de Castro 118 ❶ 963 74 66 65 ❶ www.restaurantelasucursal.com ❶ 14.00–16.00, 21.00–23.00, closed Sat lunch & Sun ❶ Metro: Turia; bus: 5, 95

BARS

Café Lisboa Despite the generous terrace in the square shaded by an olive tree, you'll be lucky to get a seat at the weekend or during a football match in this popular bar. Cocktails, wine and beer fuel the exuberant crowd. ❷ Pl. Doctor Collado 9 ❶ 963 91 94 84 ● 09.00–02.00 Ⓝ Metro: Angel Guimerá; bus: 4, 6, 7, 9, 11

Café Sant Jaume Tourists and locals flock here for the relaxed atmosphere during the week and lively chart music at the weekends. ❷ C/Caballeros 51 ❶ 963 91 24 01 ● 11.30–02.00 Ⓝ Metro: Angel Guimerá; bus: 5B, 7

Finnegans As close as you will get to a real Irish pub in Valencia, with dark wood panelling on the walls, Guinness in the glasses and frequent live music. ❷ Pl. de la Reina 19 ❶ 963 91 05 03 ● 12.30–01.00 Sun–Thur, 12.30–03.00 Fri & Sat Ⓝ Metro: Colón; bus: 4, 6

Johnny Maracas A hideously named Latin bar, with fish tanks under the bar, where professional types drink rum cocktails and dance to salsa beats. ❷ C/Caballeros 39 ❶ 963 91 52 66 ● 19.00–03.00 Ⓝ Metro: Angel Guimerá; bus: 5B, 7, 81

CLUBS

Bolsería Hang out with the beautiful people in this glass-and-chrome interior, and dance to funk and disco – you might even catch a fashion show. ❷ C/Bolsería 41 ❶ 963 91 89 03 Ⓦ www.bolseriavalencia.com ● 19.00–03.30 Ⓝ Metro: Angel Guimerá; bus: 5B, 7, 81

🔺 *Many bars around Plaza de la Reina spill out onto the streets*

Disco City Funk, retro-disco and ethnic sounds are on the DJ's menu in this all-night club in the Carmen district. ❸ C/Pintor Zariñena 16 ❶ 963 91 41 51 ❷ 24.00–07.30 Thur–Sat, closed Sun–Wed ❿ Metro: Angel Guimerá, Turia; bus: 5B, 7, 81, N4

Fox Congo House, R 'n' B and garage keep the party going in this exotically styled club with a huge onyx bar. Dress to impress at the weekend because the bouncers are picky. ❸ C/Caballeros 35 ❶ 963 91 85 67 ⓦ wwwfoxcongo.com ❷ 19.00–02.00 Tues–Wed, 19.00–03.30 Thur–Sat, closed Sun & Mon ❿ Metro: Angel Guimerá; bus: 5B

CINEMA

ABC Park Just off Calle Colón, this is the best cinema to hit if you're looking for an English-language movie. ❸ C/Roger de Lauria 21 ❶ 902 26 02 62 ⓦ www.cinesabc.com ❿ Metro: Colón; bus: 13, 14, 15, 35, 62

Port & parkland

While old Valencia has some of Europe's most beautiful medieval buildings, the city is not trapped in the past. The astonishing, white buildings that make up La Ciutat de les Arts i de les Ciències (City of Arts and Sciences, see page 90), built over the last decade or so, are awe-inspiring, and the development of the port from a neglected suburb into the venue for the 2007 America's Cup and the Formula 1 urban circuit has transformed the city's beach areas.

Valencia also boasts a remarkable amount of green space and has the perfect climate to make full use of it. The largest park meanders across the city from east to west along the old path of the Turia River (see page 100), and there are many more open areas that are full of shady spots just made for siestas. This extensive network of greenery provides a cool oasis in the summer heat, and if you want to combine relaxation with education, the unique Bioparc Valencia (see page 90) is a must.

These and many more sights outside the Old City are easy to explore using the metro, trams or buses. Bikes are ideal for discovering the parks, and a lot of the sights are within easy walking distance.

SIGHTS & ATTRACTIONS

Wouldn't it be fantastic to round off a session of heavy-duty sightseeing with a bit of sunbathing or a refreshing paddle? Here, you can: outside the Old City, you'll find plenty that's worth investigating. The bold modernity of the architecture sets up a nice contrast, and there's a real sense of excitement around the striking

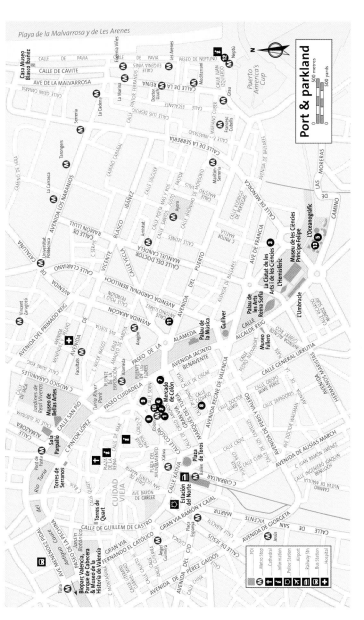

City of Arts and Sciences complex, which is seen as an emblem of Valencia's future success. And when you're ready for the beach, it's less than 20 minutes on a tram.

Bioparc Valencia

The rainforest in Valencia? Of course. This unique zoo at the far end of the Parque de Cabecera opened its doors to the general public at the end of February 2008. There are three thematic sections, reflecting the three major rainforest zones in the world – Africa, the Americas and Southeast Asia. One of the highlights of the park is the Kitum Cave, a copy of the cave by the same name in Kenya which was excavated by elephants looking for salt. ❸ Av. Pío Baroja 3 Ⓦ www.bioparcvalencia.es 🕙 10.00 – check website for closing times which vary per season Ⓝ Metro: Nou d'Octubre; bus: 7, 17, 29, 61, 81, 95. Admission charge

La Ciutat de les Arts i de les Ciències (City of Arts and Sciences)

At the river's eastern end stands this futuristic development of curvaceous white concrete, steel and glass buildings which reflect the bright Mediterranean light and are visible from around the city. Its aim is to combine culture and science to educate and entertain people of all ages; to a significant extent, the architecture alone would achieve that without any help from what lies within. The internationally acclaimed Valencian architect Santiago Calatrava designed all but one of the five sensational structures (L'Hemisfèric, Museu de les Ciències Príncipe Filipe, L'Oceanogràfic, Palau de les Arts Reina Sofía and L'Umbracle) and his creations signal that the city is ambitious for its future, as well as being proud of its past. ❸ Av. Autopista del Saler 3 ❶ 902 10 00 31 Ⓦ www.cac.es 🕙 10.00–19.00 Ⓝ Metro: Alameda; bus: 19, 35, 40, 95. Admission charge

◓ *L'Hemisfèric sits in a pool close to the Palau de les Arts Reina Sofía*

◢ *The art nouveau ticket hall at Estación del Norte*

Estación del Norte (North Train Station)

Chances are, if you arrived in Valencia by train this was the first building you saw – and what a place to start. One of the city's architectural gems, this building was completed in 1917 and was designed by Demetrio Ribes in the *modernista* (art nouveau) style. The ticket hall is decorated with colourful fragments of broken tiles (*trencadís*), as is traditional in this region, and if you look closely you'll find the hall is lined with the words 'Bon Voyage' in as many languages as would fit. ➌ C/Xátiva 24 ➊ 902 24 02 02 Ⓦ www.renfe.es Ⓝ Metro: Xátiva; bus: 5, 19, 35

L'Hemisfèric

Marooned in the centre of a turquoise pool, the white dome is cocooned in a movable glass shell, which can wink like a human eye. The inside of the dome is used as a projection surface for an IMAX cinema, Planetarium and Laserium, with a range of shows to keep everyone amused for hours. ➌ Av. Autopista del Saler 3 ➊ 902 10 00 31 Ⓦ www.cac.es Ⓝ Metro: Alameda; bus: 19, 35, 40, 95. Admission charge

Jardín Botánico (Botanic Gardens)

Located just beyond the Old City's Quart towers, the historic Botanic Gardens are the perfect place to relax and wander through some amazing plant collections. Those from cooler climates will marvel at the huge cactus and succulent garden and the open conservatory, known as '*L'Umbracle*', which shelters plants from bright sunlight. ➌ C/Quart 80 ➊ 963 15 68 00 Ⓦ www.jardibotanic.org ➍ 10.00–18.00 Nov–Feb, 10.00–19.00 Mar & Oct, 10.00–20.00 Apr & Sept, 10.00–21.00 May–Aug Ⓝ Metro: Angel Guimerá, Turia; bus: 1, 2, 5, 7, 22

Jardines de Real Viveros (Royal Gardens & Zoo)

Cross the Turia River Park from the Old City, over the Puente del Real, and you will see the gates to the Royal Gardens, once the site of Valencia's Royal Palace. Today it is a charming, shady space, full of trees, fountains, paths and clipped hedges. ⓐ C/San Pío V
ⓘ 963 525 478 ext. 4304 ⓒ 08.00–sunset ⓜ Metro: Alameda, Pont de Fusta; bus: 5B, 32, 95

Mercado de Colón

This open-sided *modernista* market building was designed in 1914 and is decorated with *trencadis* (broken ceramic mosaic)

ⓐ *Art nouveau Mercado de Colón houses cafés and bars these days*

VALENCIA'S PORT & THE AMERICA'S CUP

Although the people of Valencia are fiercely proud of their city, even they were a little surprised when it was chosen to host the prestigious America's Cup race in 2007, against competition from such fashionable rivals as Barcelona. They rose to the challenge, however, and the city naturally focused its plans on the port area that it had ignored for so long. Consequently, this area is well worth a visit for those with any interest in sailing or the America's Cup phenomenon.

Many of the run-down residential areas near the port have seen significant redevelopment, as has the port itself. This is now the base for all the America's Cup teams, each of which has its own building, and old *modernista* warehouses have been transformed into an area for spectators. There is also a visitor centre, with no admission charge, describing the history of the competition. Even the entrance to the port has been moved to improve access for the racing yachts. As part of an ambitious plan to improve the transport system, an extension of Metro line 5 now links the port and airport. ❸ Av. Manuel Soto ⓦ www.valenciaport.com/, www.americascup.com ⓝ Metro: Neptú; bus: 3, 4, 23, 30

that shows a charming depiction of a grape harvest. Following restoration, this is no longer home to a bustling local market, but now accommodates cafés, restaurants and a few flower stalls. The building in particular should not be missed. ❸ C/Jorge Juan 19 ⓝ Metro: Colón; bus: 2, 3, 5, 12, 13

Museu de les Ciències Príncipe Felipe (Science Museum)

This impressive building, reminiscent of a whale's ribcage, is home to the popular Science Museum. Visitors are encouraged to interact with the exhibits, which range from giant pendulums and a model of the International Space Station, to an entertaining biology exhibition that focuses on genetics. Most explanations are translated into English and guided tours are also available.
📍 Av. Autopista del Saler 7 ☎ 902 10 00 31 🌐 www.cac.es 🕐 10.00–19.00
Ⓜ Metro: Alameda; bus: 19, 35, 40, 95. Admission charge

Museo de la Historia de Valencia (Valencia History Museum)

Learn about the 22 centuries of Valencia's history by hearing about and watching the stories of its inhabitants. No dull list of dates and events this, but real people showing life in the past. The visit starts in modern Valencia, and then the visitor is placed into a time machine and sent back to the days of the Romans before zipping chronologically back to today. 📍 C/Valencia 42 (Mislata) (Continuation of the Paseo de la Pechina) ☎ 963 70 11 05
🌐 www.valencia.es/mhv 🕐 10.00–14.00, 16.30–20.30 Tues–Sat, closed Sun & Mon Ⓜ Metro: 9 de Octubre; bus: 3, 7, 17, 81, 95

L'Oceanogràfic

The architect Felix Candela's design is an amazing aquarium complex, made up of lagoons above ground and aquaria below, which illustrate the world's marine ecosystems. Marvel at a huge diversity of shimmering fish, sharks and rays as you walk through tunnels on the beds of the Oceans and Temperate & Tropical aquaria. There is also a dolphinarium with regular shows, while the Arctic

● *The dramatic exterior of the Science Museum*

and Antarctic sections are home to beluga whales, walruses and penguins. ❷ Junta de Murs i Valls ❶ 902 10 00 31 Ⓦ www.cac.es Ⓛ 10.00–18.00 Sun–Fri, 10.00–20.00 Sat & public holidays Ⓜ Metro: Alameda; bus: 19, 35, 40, 95. Admission charge

Playa de la Malvarrosa and Playa de les Arenes (Malvarrosa Beach/Arenas Beach)

It's handy having a beautiful beach on your doorstep. When the strain – they call it positive stress – of shopping and sightseeing begins to tell, all you need to do is head for the city's fabulous stretch of golden sand. On the beach you'll find volleyball courts, play areas and blocks with toilets and showers, as well as a long promenade where those who don't want to get sand in their shoes can take a stroll. The seemingly countless restaurants that line Playa de les Arenes could easily take care of your dining requirements for your entire visit, and are great places in which to sample proper paella. On the short walk between the metro and the beach you will pass colourful rows of old fishermen's houses. It could be that this entire area will be redeveloped as part of a regeneration scheme, so treat yourself to a visit before it gets a makeover. ❷ Paseo Marítimo Ⓜ Metro: Mediterrani, Neptú; tram: Les Arenes, Eugenia Viñes; bus: 20, 21, 22, 23, 32

Plaza de Toros (Bullring)

Right next to the Estación del Norte is the 19th-century bullring, built in a neoclassical style from brick and wood. Although the popularity of bullfighting is on the wane among young Valencians the events are still incredibly popular, especially during *Las Fallas*

Ⓞ *L'Oceanogràfic is just one of the five buildings of the City of Arts and Sciences*

in March and in July. Tickets can be hard to come by, but may be purchased from the adjacent Museo Taurino (Bullfighting Museum), which is also worth visiting. Entrance to the bullring for visitors only through the museum. ❷ Pasaje Dr Serra 10 ❶ 963 88 37 38 ❶ www.museotaurinovalencia.es ❶ 10.00–20.00 Tues–Sun, closed Mon ❷ Metro: Xátiva; bus: 5, 19, 35

Turia River Park & Parque de Cabecera (Headwaters Park)

Valencia's catastrophic flood in 1957 spelt the end for the River Turia's ancient course through the city; it was safely diverted to the southwest of the historic centre. Today, in its place, there is a fabulous, popular park, known as 'the river' to locals, which is packed with shady groves of trees, fountains, cycle paths and sports facilities.

There are playgrounds dotted along the park's length, but by far the best is Gulliver, towards the eastern end, not far from the City of Arts and Sciences. Someone had the bright idea of letting the children play at being Lilliputians by clambering all over the model of a giant lying on the ground. Poor Gulliver never gets a moment's peace, because he is covered in fantastic ramps and slides.

At the western end of 'the river' is the Parque de Cabecera, opened in 2003. This landscaped area, designed to echo the local Albufera marsh, has a large, naturalistic lake, home to ducks and goldfish. Fantastic, swan-shaped pedaloes can be hired from outside the terrace café, which sells drinks and snacks, and there is a small amphitheatre set into the side of the hill, where there are evening performances. There is also a great playground for children. ❷ Enter from the end of Av. Manuel de Falla or from the Turia River Park ❷ Metro: Nou d'Octubre; bus: 7, 95

● *The Turia River no longer flows under this bridge, just a pool of water*

L'Umbracle

Artfully disguising the car park underneath, *L'Umbracle*, an open conservatory of white hoops, sheltering a palm-lined promenade and attractive gardens from the bright sunlight, forms the entrance to the City of Arts and Sciences. Eventually climbing plants will clamber up the structure, providing welcome shade while visitors take in the great view of the whole complex. There are 50 plant species from the Valencia region and an outdoor art gallery with sculptures by contemporary artists. ⓐ Av. Autopista del Saler 5 ⓣ 902 10 00 31 ⓦ www.cac.es ⓝ Metro: Alameda; bus: 19, 35, 40, 95

Valencia Bikes

These three-hour guided bike tours of the major sights within and outside the Old City are a great way to get your bearings. The price includes bike hire and refreshments. ⓐ Tour leaves from Paseo

de la Pechina 32 ❶ 963 851 740 ⓦ www.valenciabikes.com
🕓 10.00–13.00 Sat. Admission charge for tour

Valencia Bus Turistic
Buy a ticket for the open-top bus and it will take you to the
major sights outside the Old City, including the IVAM Centre Julio
González (Valencian Institute of Modern Art, see page 72) and the
City of Arts and Sciences (see page 90) and provide a multilingual
audio guide. The bus leaves from Plaza de la Reina and stops at five
major points throughout the city. ❷ Pl. de la Reina ❶ 963 41 44 00
ⓦ www.valenciabusturistic.com ⓝ Metro: Angel Guimerá;
bus: 4, 6, 7, 9, 11

CULTURE

Those in search of culture need not think that it is confined to the
Old City; in fact what is arguably the city's best museum, the Museo
de Bellas Artes (Museum of Fine Arts), faces the historic centre
across the Turia River Park.

Casa Museo Blasco Ibañéz (House of Blasco Ibañéz)
The works of Valencian writer Vicente Blasco Ibañéz (1867–1928)
are now largely forgotten. However, the writer is still remembered
in street names and his house in the Malvarrosa district has been
turned into a museum. The majority of his works are on display
here, and the house is also used for temporary exhibitions. There
are guided tours. ❷ C/Isabel de Villena 149 ❶ 963 52 54 78 ext. 2568
🕓 10.00–14.00, 16.30–20.30 Tues–Sat, 10.00–15.00 Sun & public
holidays, closed Mon ⓝ Tram: la Cadena; bus: 1, 2, 19, 32. Admission
charge (except on Sun & public holidays)

Museo de Bellas Artes (Museum of Fine Arts)

One of Spain's most important art museums, and certainly a must on any visit to Valencia. The building's blue-tiled dome rises over the Turia River Park, just a hop across Puente Trinidad from the Old City. Inside, the treasures begin with an almost overwhelming collection of 13th- to 15th-century religious art that drops heavy hints about Valencia's wealth in the Middle Ages. In contrast are the grotesque faces of Bosch's *Triptych of the Passion*, which hangs in the next hall.

Move to the first floor and you will find works by Valencians Ribalta and Ribera, as well as El Greco's luminous depiction of St John the Baptist and Goya's portrait of one of his mistresses. On the second floor are beautiful paintings by the Valencian Impressionist Sorolla and Expressionist Pinazo. Don't miss the beautiful *Patio del Embajador Vich*, one of the finest examples of Renaissance art in Valencia. ⓐ C/San Pío V 9 ⓣ 963 87 03 00 ⓦ www.cult.gva.es/mbav ⓝ Tram: Pont de Fusta; bus: 1, 5B, 6, 8, 95

Museo Fallero (Fallas Museum)

For those who can't make the *Fallas* fiesta in March (see page 12), this museum provides an opportunity to see the collection of *ninots* (*papier-mâché* caricature figures) that have been rescued from its fiery clutches. The collection began in 1934 and thankfully does not include any of the deafening firecrackers of the fiesta itself. ⓐ Av. San José Artisano 17 ⓣ 963 52 54 78 ext. 4625 ⓦ www.fallas.com/museo.htm ⓛ 10.00–14.00, 16.30–20.30 Tues–Sat, 10.00–15.00 Sun & public holidays, closed Mon ⓝ Bus: 13, 14, 18, 35, 95. Admission charge

Palau de les Arts Reina Sofía (Opera House)

Santiago Calatrava's opera house opened in late 2005. Valencia has no history of opera, so it may take some time for a mature programme to develop, but things have got off to an encouraging start.

The impressive Main Hall, with its curved surfaces and white concrete, is unashamedly modern, as are the text screens that allow the libretto to be followed in several languages by an audience of 1,800. Another venue with the same capacity is the Amphitheatre that's also found here. The smaller Master Room is specially designed to host small musical ensembles. ➌ Autopista del Saler 1 ➊ 961 97 58 00 ⓦ www.lesarts.com ⓛ 10.00–18.00 Mon–Sat, closed Sun ⓜ Metro: Alameda; bus: 19, 35, 40, 95

Palau de la Música (Concert Hall)

Constructed in 1987 among the beautiful gardens and fountains of the Turia River Park, the Palau de la Música was intended to encourage culture in the city; its incredible popularity today shows that it has done just that.

The concert hall's diverse programme of jazz and classical performances, as well as opera, ballet and musicals, means that there should be something to suit all tastes. ➌ Paseo de la Alameda 30 ➊ 963 37 50 20 ⓦ www.palaudevalencia.com ⓛ variable according to event ⓜ Metro: Aragón; bus: 95

Sala Parpalló

Housed in the 15th-century Real Monasterio de la Trinidad (Royal Monastery of the Trinity), this gallery opened in 1980 and was one of the first public spaces to show the work of modern and contemporary artists. After more than 25 years it is still dedicated to new ways of expression of, in particular, Valencian artists. ➌ C/Alboraya 5 ➊ 963 61 44 15 ⓦ www.salaparpallo.es ⓛ 10.00–14.00, 16.00–20.00 Tues–Sat, 10.00–14.00 Sun, closed Mon ⓜ Tram: Pont de Fusta; bus: 1, 5B, 6, 8, 11

RETAIL THERAPY

The main shopping streets here actually run off the Old City's biggest shopping mecca, Calle Colón, so it is easy to combine a little retail therapy in both areas. The roads surrounding the beautiful Mercado de Colón have the greatest concentration of stores while the various delights of both Calle Jorge Juan and Calle Sorní encourage severe GBH of the credit card.

Begoña de Sobrecueva A stylish shoe emporium, with everything a girl could need, from glamorous heels to practical boots. ⓐ C/Sorní 28 ⓣ 963 52 96 42 ⓛ 10.00–14.00, 17.00–20.30 Mon–Fri, 10.30–14.00, 17.00–20.00 Sat, closed Sun ⓜ Metro: Colón; bus: 4, 10

Furla A designer boutique dedicated to leather goods, including great bags, shoes, belts and every accessory imaginable. ⓐ C/Sorní 1 ⓣ 963 52 36 73 ⓦ www.furla.com ⓛ 10.30–13.30, 16.30–20.30 Mon–Sat, closed Sun ⓜ Metro: Colón; bus: 4, 10

Manglano Local ham (in particular Serrano ham) is a speciality at this delicatessen. ⓐ Mercado Colón, downstairs, C/Jorge Juan 19 ⓣ 963 52 88 54 ⓛ 08.00–21.00 Mon–Sat, closed Sun ⓜ Metro: Colón; bus: 2, 3, 5, 12, 13

Mestalla Flea Market This vast market takes place every Sunday in the square next to the Valencia football stadium, close to the city centre. Seek and you will find antiques, paintings and all kinds of quirky collectables, so do as the Valencians do and hunt down a bargain. ⓐ Av. de Aragón 09.00–14.00 Sun ⓜ Metro: Aragón; bus: 10, 12, 41, 80

Siete Mares This rather upmarket shop stocks classy women's collections, including footwear and accessories. C/Sorní 20 & 22 963 34 17 27 10.00–14.00, 16.30–20.30 Mon–Fri, 10.30–14.00, 17.00–20.30 Sat, closed Sun Metro: Colón; bus: 4, 10

Sinéquanone Smart and chic French clothes without the designer pricetag. C/Jorge Juan 6 963 94 35 21 www.sinequanone.com 10.30–20.30 Mon–Thur, until 21.00 Fri & Sat, closed Sun Metro: Colón; bus: 2, 3, 5, 12, 13

Tommy Hilfiger The famous all-American look for men and women. C/Jorge Juan 14 963 53 28 29 www.tommy.com 10.00–21.00 Mon–Sat, closed Sun Metro: Colón; bus: 5, 32

Yacaré If shoes are your thing you could be lost for hours in one of this shoe-obsessed city's best stores. C/Jorge Juan 8 963 51 18 02 10.00–21.00 Mon–Sat, closed Sun Metro: Colón; bus: 5, 32

Zara Home Trendy interior goods, such as bed linen and cosmetics, by this name best known in the UK for clothes. C/Jorge Juan 15 963 51 32 52 www.zarahome.com 10.00–21.00 Mon–Sat, closed Sun Metro: Colón; bus: 5, 32

TAKING A BREAK

Although there is not the concentration of cafés and bars here that there is in the Old City, there are still plenty dotted around where you can pick up a coffee or lunch when sightseeing or shopping. Many have street terraces, where you can soak up the sun and

⬥ *The beautiful Mercado de Colón stands at the heart of the shopping area*

also serve tapas throughout the day if you need some extra energy.
The stylish cafés in Mercado de Colón are the in-places to be seen
sipping a cappuccino.

Casaní Patisseria £ ❶ Take a break from shopping for a reviving
coffee and indulgent cake, to take away or eat on a stool inside.
🅐 C/Jorge Juan 12 (off Calle Colón) 🕽 963 52 57 20 🕒 07.30–14.30,
16.30–21.00 Mon–Sat, closed Sun 🇳 Metro: Colón; bus: 5, 32

Coffee House £ ❷ The elegant surroundings of the
Mercado de Colón are perfect to enjoy a coffee, perhaps with
a decadent dash of liqueur. 🅐 Mercado Colón, C/Jorge Juan 19
🕽 963 94 21 61 🇼 www.coffeehouse.es 🕒 09.00–22.00 Mon–Thur,
09.00–24.00 Fri, 10.00–01.00 Sat, 10.00–23.00 Sun
🇳 Metro: Colón; bus: 2, 3, 5, 12, 13

El Corte Inglés £ ❸ The restaurant on the top floor of
this department store is great for coffee or lunch, while the
basement supermarket is packed with delicious picnic delicacies.
🅐 C/Pintor Maella 37 🕽 963 35 05 00 🇼 www.elcorteingles.es
🕒 10.00–22.00 Mon–Sat, closed Sun 🇳 Bus: 19, 20

Mon Orxata £ ❹ This is the place if you fancy healthy,
organic *horchata*. They also sell chocolate, cocktails, juices and
ice cream. 🅐 Mercado Colón, C/Jorge Juan 19 🕽 961 86 15 61
🇼 www.monorxata.com 🕒 08.30–22.00 🇳 Metro: Colón;
bus: 2, 3, 5, 12, 13

Restaurante Oceanos £ ❺ The best lunch option in the
aquarium complex, serving good burgers and salads next to the

pelican lake. ⓐ L'Oceanogràfic, Junta de Murs i Valls ⓣ 961 97 55 63 ⓛ 20.30–01.00 Thur–Sat, closed Sun–Wed ⓜ Metro: Alameda; bus: 19, 35, 40, 95

Suprem £ ⓞ This is a good place to have a quick coffee and a fresh baguette. Also try the chilled coffee or *horchata*. ⓐ Pl. de los Pinazos 6 (off Calle Colón) ⓣ 606 67 27 19 ⓛ 08.00–21.30 Mon–Fri, 09.00–21.30 Sat, closed Sun ⓜ Metro: Colón; bus: 5, 10, 13, 3, 81

AFTER DARK

There are a number of nightlife hotspots that are worth seeking out. Head down to the beach in summer for bustling seafood restaurants and some increasingly cool and late-opening bars. The student haunts around Avenida Blasco Ibáñez, close to the university, are tourist-friendly and good fun.

RESTAURANTS
La Barrica £ ⓦ Bustling and friendly, this place serves delicious and substantial tapas, with a good range of wines by the glass. ⓐ C/Serrano Morales 3 ⓣ 963 34 81 32 ⓛ 09.00–17.00, 21.00–01.00 Mon–Fri, 19.00–01.00 Sat, closed Sun ⓜ Metro: Alameda, Colón; bus: 2, 12

Inbocca £–££ ⓞ Classy restaurant where you can enjoy creative dishes that taste good enough to have been made at home (assuming that whoever does the cooking at your place is a top Spanish chef). After dinner you can dance the night away. ⓐ C/Conde Altea 22 ⓣ 963 35 53 47 ⓦ www.inbocca.es ⓛ 14.00–16.30, 21.00–01.30 Tues–Sat, closed Sun & Mon ⓜ Metro: Colón; bus: 41, 3

◆ The stylish bar at the Inbocca restaurant

Albacar ££ ❾ A crisp, bright, family-run restaurant with a seasonal menu that makes the most of local produce. Traditional rice and fish dishes, served with flare, are the most popular option. ❸ C/Sorní 35 ❶ 963 95 10 05 ❺ 13.00–15.30, 21.00–23.30 Mon–Fri, 21.00–23.30 Sat, closed Sun Ⓝ Metro: Colón; bus: 4, 10, N8

Bamboo de Colón ££ ❿ In the lower level of Mercado de Colón, this trendy spot is in a handy location for shoppers. It has an Italian-influenced menu and set lunches at a convenient price. ❸ C/Jorge Juan 19 ❶ 963 53 03 37 Ⓦ www.elaltocatering.com ❺ 13.30–16.00, 20.30–23.30 Mon–Thur, 13.30–16.00, 21.00–24.00 Fri, 14.00–16.00, 21.00–24.00 Sat & Sun Ⓝ Metro: Colón; bus: 2, 3, 5, 12, 13

La Cocina de China ££ ⓫ Unlike the more 'traditional' Chinese restaurants in Valencia, the dishes here are creative and made with homegrown vegetables. The interior is very chic with minimalist oriental decoration. ❸ C/Antonio Suárez 23 ❶ 963 60 46 96 ❺ 13.30–16.00, 08.30–24.00 Ⓝ Metro: Aragón; bus: 90

La Pepica ££ ⓬ Down by the beach, this Valencian institution has served paella to the Spanish Royals, Ernest Hemingway and Pelé. Try and get a seat on the terrace with a sea view. ❸ Paseo de Neptuno 2, 6 & 8 ❶ 963 71 03 66 Ⓦ www.lapepica.com ❺ 13.00–16.00, 20.30–23.00 Mon–Sat, 13.00–16.00 Sun Ⓝ Metro: Neptú; bus: 20, 22, 23

Restaurante Submarino £££ ⓭ A spectacular setting with views into L'Oceanogràfic aquarium, but don't let the marine life distract from the exquisite and varied meat and fish dishes. ❸ L'Oceanogràfic ❶ 961 97 55 65 Ⓦ www.grupo-jbl.com ❺ 13.00–15.30, 21.00–22.30 Ⓝ Bus: 25, 95, 15 ❶ Reservations recommended

● *A favourite place for paella, right by the beach*

BARS

Café Alameda The terrace of this art café is open year-round and is a great place to enjoy a cocktail while listening to live music. House music at weekends. ⓐ Paseo de la Alameda 6 ⓣ 963 44 83 96 ⓦ www.caféalameda.com ⓛ 15.00–04.00 ⓝ Metro: Alameda; bus: 5B, 6, 8, 11, N3

Café Lola You'll have a blast at this bar, where good music from all eras is guaranteed to get you going. Good prices, good drinks, good times. ⓐ C/Actriz Encarna Máñez 1 ⓣ 963 55 30 97 ⓦ www.cafélola.org ⓛ 17.00–04.00 ⓝ Metro: Amistad; bus: 18, 89, 90, N10

Gandhara Head to the beach and try this atmospheric, Thai-inspired bar that's full of incense and lone drinkers during the week and packed with party-punters at the weekend. ⓐ C/Eugenia Viñes 225 ⓣ 963 71 00 25 ⓦ www.gandharaterraza.com ⓛ 23.00–04.00 ⓜ Metro: Neptú; bus: 20, 21, 22, 23, 30, 32

Gran Café Designed by the Valencian artist and architect Javier Mariscal, this place still has its original bar. *Agua de Valencia* is a speciality, and the art on the wall is by local painters. ⓐ Gran Vía Marqués de Turia 76 ⓣ 963 60 78 60 ⓛ 18.30–01.30 ⓜ Metro: Colón; bus: 41, 79

The Hops Inn A good attempt at recreating an English pub; that substance that's missing when you sit outside is called rain. ⓐ C/Cirilo Amorós 73 ⓣ 963 94 16 33 ⓛ 12.00–01.30 Mon–Wed, 12.00–03.30 Thur–Sat, closed Sun ⓜ Metro: Colón; bus: 35, N1

Rocafull Café If you fancy checking out the student bars, head to this colourful spot, half-way between the Old City and the beach, for cheap drinks, a good range of beer and a relaxed atmosphere. ⓐ Pl. Xuquer 14 ⓣ 963 32 09 54 ⓦ www.rocafull.tk ⓛ 15.30–02.00 ⓜ Metro: Aragón; bus: 31, 41, 71, 81, N1

CLUBS
Black Note Club Hosts great live music almost every night at 23.30 and 01.00. You'll find jazz, blues, soul and Latin groups and an appreciative audience of locals and tourists. ⓐ C/Polo y Peyrolón 15 ⓣ 963 93 36 63 ⓦ www.blacknoteclub.com ⓛ 22.00–03.30 Mon–Sat, closed Sun ⓜ Metro: Aragón; bus: 79, 32. Admission charge for some events

Giorgio & Enrico There are no fewer than six spaces in which to dance, chill out and have fun in this club. Pl. del Canónigo 1 (Benimamet) 963 45 50 42 24.00–08.00 Fri & Sat, closed Sun–Thur www.giorgioenrico.com Metro: Benimamet

La Indiana A classy club that plays house, funk and Latin beats. Also hosts live music and dance on Thursdays. Boy, are those bouncers fussy. C/San Vicente Mártir 97 Offices 963 84 50 51 www.laindiana.com 24.00–06.00 Thur–Sat, closed Sun–Wed Metro: Plaza España; bus: 70, 71, 72, N4, N5. Admission charge

CINEMA

Babel A great little art-house cinema, just off Avenida Aragón, that shows international films in their original version (not always English). Check the website for screenings. C/Vicente Sancho Tello 10 963 62 67 95 www.cinesalbatrosbabel.com Metro: Aragón; bus: 10, 12, 79

Away from the city, there are charming seaside towns to discover

OUT OF TOWN
trips

South of the city

Take the Nazaret–Oliva road south out of the city, and within minutes you'll be passing fields full of orange trees, vegetables and rice. A perfect day-trip destination is the tranquil Albufera lake (see page 118), a nature reserve favoured by all kinds of birds and wildlife and a carefully controlled source of water for traditional rice cultivation. Take a boat trip with a local fisherman, then head to the village of El Palmar (see page 120), on what was once an island in the lake, where many restaurants serve paellas and other rice dishes.

When the heat of the city gets too much, the golden stretches of sand at Pinedo (see page 121), El Saler (see page 123) and La Devesa (see page 122) are the best places to cool off and escape the crowds. No more than 16 km (10 miles) from the city centre, many Valencians treat these beaches, particularly El Saler, as summer retreats and will often commute to work from flats there. Consequently the facilities in this area are good, with bars, restaurants, hotels and the well-known El Saler Golf Course all catering to locals and tourists, so you may even decide to base yourself outside Valencia to make the most of your break.

If you would like to take a structured tour to learn about the area, there are guided bicycle and boat tours run by **Port Albufera** (❸ C/29 Parc-536 Industrial Estate of Catarroja ❶ 961 26 25 31 ⓦ www.portalbufera.com. Admission charge), which explain local history, traditions and wildlife.

GETTING THERE

Depending on whether you want a quick tour of the area or a chance to travel more independently, there are a number of transport options from Valencia. The most flexible of these is to hire a car for a day, or

ALBUFERA LAKE

Since the Moors introduced rice cultivation to this area, the Albufera lake (actually a freshwater lagoon) has been shrinking; farmers add soil to the water to create rice paddies, a practice which, over the centuries, has reclaimed thousands of hectares of land. Rice crops still line the roadside, but the lake has been protected as a nature reserve since 1986 and is home to many species of birds, both native and migratory, as well as other flora and fauna. Local fishermen still catch eels, but have diversified and will take visitors on boat trips around the mirror-like lake, with its strange reed-lined channels (look for *paseos en barca* signs by the roadside). ⓐ Embarcadero de la Gola del Pujo, road CV500 ⓣ 680 504 464 ⓦ www.albufera.com ⓛ every day, except in bad weather

longer, to allow you to explore as you please, but the short distance from the city also makes taxis a viable option; just remember to take a taxi-firm's number to arrange your return trip.

Local buses, run by **Autocares Herca** (☎ 963 491 250), depart from Gran Vía Germanías (near Calle Sueca) and Plaza Cánovas del Castillo to El Saler town and beach hourly between 07.00 and 21.00. The **Albufera Bus Turistic** (🌐 www.valenciabusturistic.com/albufera/html) also provides a quick, two-hour tour from Plaza de la Reina, around the lake, nature reserve and El Palmar, including a boat trip and an audio-guide in eight languages (ask at tourist information office for timetable).

Due to the proximity to the city, cycling is a very feasible way of getting around, not to mention a good way to appreciate the peace and quiet and spot wildlife.

◆ *Eel fishermen get to work on Albufera lake*

SIGHTS & ATTRACTIONS

El Palmar

There are some 30 restaurants in this little island village, but the huge numbers of loyal visitors from the city ensure that they all do a good trade, particularly at the weekend. After you have eaten, take a stroll down to the water to see the long, flat, brightly

🔻 *Typical of El Palmar are distinct thatched* barracas *houses*

painted fishing boats and find one of their owners to take you out onto the lake. Boat trips with dinner on the water can even be arranged (see page 118).

Pinedo Beach

Just 3 km (2 miles) south of where the diverted Turia River reaches the sea, this beach is extremely close to the city and, indeed, its huge commercial port, but is still sufficiently clean to have been

awarded a Blue Flag. It is not as rural as beaches further south, but has fine sand and good facilities, including lifeguards on duty from 11.00 until 19.00 in summer.

Playa de la Devesa

For a truly unspoilt beach, this has to be one of the best, with clean water and 5 km (3 miles) of golden sand. Still only 16 km (10 miles) from the city centre, the beach is backed by the dunes and pine forest of the same name, which are good to explore.

Raco de l'Olla Information Centre

Turn off the Nazaret–Oliva road to El Palmar to find this small exhibition centre and popular bird-watching spot. The unsympathetic concrete building houses displays showing how a crazy plan to turn the area into a leisure park in the 1950s and 1960s came close to destroying its natural beauty. The main road that ploughs through the sensitive pine woodland and dunes remains, but almost all traces of the horse-racing track and tennis courts are gone. Although there is no English explanation, the photographs speak for themselves.

Climb to the top of the observation tower for panoramic views over the lake and surrounding countryside back to Valencia. Then wander through the pine trees to the shed by the water, which acts as a hide, and test your bird-spotting skills. The lake has thousands of resident ducks and white egrets, as well as migrant flamingos and booted eagles.

There are toilets in the Information Centre. ❷ C/Palmar 21 ❶ 961 62 73 45 ❸ 09.00–14.00 ❶ Afternoon opening times given are subject to changes due to weather conditions, please call prior to visit

El Saler

A mere 12 km (7 miles) from the city centre, the town of El Saler, set back from 5 km (3 miles) of wonderful sandy beach, is a viable base for a holiday combining the city lights of Valencia and some proper relaxation. Sadly, it did not escape the phase of coastal tower-block building that Spain went through in the 1960s, but it is still an appealing place, with a Blue Flag award, good hotels, restaurants and bars. Public buses run to Valencia frequently, but some of the larger hotels offer free shuttle buses too, so keep your eyes open. In summer the *Gabri* wind blows reliably each evening, making this a popular place for windsurfing.

The well-known golf course, Campo de Golf El Saler, next door to the *parador*, is ranked among the top 100 courses in the world and is frequently a venue for professional competitions. It is expensive for a round, with reduced rates for *parador* residents.
🅐 Parador El Saler, Av. de los Pinares 151 🅣 961 61 03 84
🅦 www.parador.es

AFTER DARK

If you find yourself in El Saler on a summer evening then you will be spoilt for choice on the beachfront for places to eat and drink. Likewise in the village of El Palmar it is almost impossible to choose between the restaurants serving typical local food, but it is an idea to book your table in advance at the weekend and to remember that not all establishments open in the evening midweek.

RESTAURANTS

Casa Carmina ££ An El Saler restaurant with a homely, local feel and some of the most lovingly prepared rice dishes in town.

🅐 Calle Embarcadero 4 🕐 961 83 02 54 🕑 13.00–18.00 Tues–Sun, closed Mon

Nou Raco ££ A slick, modern development near El Palmar, decorated with traditional tiles, next to Albufera lake. Sample a range of typical fish and rice dishes, as well as salads.
🅐 Carretera de El Palmar 21 🕐 961 62 01 72 🕑 10.00–18.00
🅘 Reservations recommended

Restaurante Bon Aire ££ The menu at this El Palmar restaurant is packed with a huge range of traditional rice dishes (not all of them paella) and also includes fresh local fish dishes.
🅐 C/Caudet 41 🕐 961 62 01 33 🆆 www.restaurantebonaire.com
🕑 13.30–16.30, 21.00–23.30

Restaurante Mateu ££ A favourite in El Palmar because of its great traditional cuisine with a Mediterranean twist. Expect the highest quality paella, fish and seafood, in a friendly atmosphere.
🅐 C/Vicente Valdobi 17 🕐 961 620 270 🕑 13.00–16.00 Sun–Thur, 13.00–16.00, 20.30–23.00 Fri & Sat 🅘 Reservation recommended at weekends

CLUBS
Bounty Saler Hosts all kinds of special events, as well as karaoke. Party into the small hours to feel-good disco and chart music.
🅐 Av. Pinares 24–26 🕐 961 83 00 18 🆆 www.bountysaler.com
🕑 24.00–03.00 Thur, 22.00–05.00 Fri, 24.00–07.00 Sat, 19.30–05.00 Sun, closed Mon–Wed. Admission charge

Puzzle A must for hardcore clubbers, this huge club has survived since 1986 by being the best and hosts international DJs, playing progressive house and techno. **ⓐ** Carretera Nazaret–Oliva, km 22, El Perelló **ⓣ** 961 77 09 35 **ⓦ** www.discotecapuzzle.com **ⓛ** 01.00–09.00 Sun, closed Mon–Sat **ⓐ** Bus: Autocares Herca bus to El Perelló from Pl. Cánovas del Castillo (last bus leaves 22.00); train: from Valencia Estación del Norte take C-1 regional line to Gandía. Admission charge

ACCOMMODATION

Camping Coll Vert £ Friendly people at this campsite close to the Pinedo beach. There is a swimming pool and activities for children. Bungalows also available. **ⓐ** Carretera del Ríu 486 (Pinedo beach) **ⓣ** 961 83 00 36 **ⓕ** 961 83 00 40 **ⓦ** www.collvertcamping.com **ⓘ** Closed from 15 Dec–15 Jan

Hotel Sidi Saler £££ A rather unattractive tower block with excellent facilities in the most amazing position, right on the beach. The hotel has its own restaurants, bars and pool and is a great base for a family holiday. **ⓐ** Playa el Saler **ⓣ** 961 61 04 11 **ⓦ** www.sidi-saler.com

Parador El Saler £££ A modern building with well-equipped rooms, each with a view of the sea or famous golf course. There is a restaurant, gym, small pool and access to a quiet stretch of beach. **ⓐ** Av. de los Pinares 151, El Saler **ⓣ** 961 61 11 86 **ⓦ** www.parador.es

North & west of the city

Pretty coastal towns, often fortified and almost all with fabulous lengths of spotless sand, are to be found to the north of Valencia. To the west there are dramatic hilltop villages within easy reach of the city.

The imposing Gothic monastery at Puig, with its fascinating array of art and books, is only a 20-minute journey away. Just a little further north, Sagunt's captivating Roman theatre and extensive medieval *castillo* (castle), along with the charming town itself, would happily fill a day's exploring.

For lovers of sun and sea, the dune-backed beaches of nearby Port de Sagunt may hold more appeal. The lively seaside town of Benicàssim, about an hour north of Valencia, is another good option for those who want to head for the beach, but really comes alive for the four-day Festival Internacional de Benicàssim (see page 128), which is a mecca for fans of live music. For more information about the festival, visit Ⓦ www.fiberfib.com

If your burning ambition is to be at the centre of a tomato-throwing battle, then burn no more and head west to the normally quiet town of Buñol on the last Wednesday in August and join in the manic festival known as *La Tomatina*.

GETTING THERE

Bus and train services to these towns are fairly cheap, frequent and easy to use and driving to them is a matter of getting onto the A-7 motorway (north) or the A-3 (west). Bus number 115 to Sagunt and Port de Sagunt leaves Valencia's Estación Central de Autobuses (see page 50) every 30 minutes from 07.00 to 22.00 (check timetable

for stops at Puig), while trains go from Valencia North Station every 20 minutes.

SIGHTS & ATTRACTIONS

Benicàssim & the FIB festival

The charming seaside town of Benicàssim is about 85 km (53 miles) north of Valencia. Its ancient fortress, long, immaculate sandy beaches and vivid nightlife make it worth visiting at any time of the year. One particular event draws the biggest crowds: the Festival Internacional de Benicàssim (FIB). For the past 11 years, music fans from all over Europe have flocked to the festival site, close to the beach, to enjoy some of the best live rock, pop and electronica acts on offer anywhere, as well as short films, dance, theatre and plenty of partying. British bands often feature heavily in the four-day line-up and recent big names have included the B-52's, The Human League and Amy Winehouse. Check the excellent and informative ⓦ www.fiberfib.com

Port de Sagunt

For those who prefer rest and relaxation to historic buildings, the long stretches of sandy beach at Port de Sagunt are the ideal alternative to its namesake, 4 km (2.5 miles) inland, and are becoming increasingly popular with visitors. The beaches, called Almardà, Corinto and Malvarrosa, are all clean, with wonderfully clear water that is great for a dip. The two towns are linked by bus 102.

● *Sagunt is a seaside town with some character*

Real Monasterio de El Puig de Santa María

Just a few kilometres north of Valencia, the town of Puig is dominated by the imposing Royal Monastery of Santa María. This grand, rectangular, Gothic building, with its four corner towers, was begun in 1588, but elements inside it date back further.

The oldest section is the sanctuary, where the 14th-century church houses a beautiful Byzantine image of the Virgin from the 6th century.

The magnificent 16th-century Gothic cloisters provide access to, among other things, an impressive hall, a fascinating collection

◗ *The Gothic monastery at Puig is the town's dominant landmark*

of 17th- and 18th-century paintings and a museum of printing, where many amazing ancient books are kept. The only way to visit the monastery is with a guided (multilingual) tour that leaves at 10.00, 11.00, 12.00, 16.00 and 17.00. This is a perfect day trip, within easy reach of the city of Valencia, with plenty of restaurants in town where you can enjoy a leisurely lunch. ⓐ Av. Virgen del Puig ⓣ 961 47 02 00 ⓛ 10.00–12.00, 16.00–18.00 Tues–Sun, closed Mon. Admission charge

Sagunt (Sagunto)

Sheltering beneath the Sierra Calderona mountains, 28 km (17 miles) north of Valencia, Sagunt is an attractive town, full of history and begging to be explored. In 219 BC, the town, then allied with Rome, endured an eight-month siege by the Carthaginians, led by Hannibal. With no rescue in sight, the citizens opted to torch the town and commit suicide rather than surrender. Following Rome's defeat of Carthage, the town's sacrifice was recognised and a fortressed city was rebuilt in its place.

One incredible survivor from this era is the Roman theatre, which was built into the side of the mountain in the 1st century and thus has exceptional acoustics. Modernisation of the amphitheatre, to allow its use as a modern venue, has caused considerable controversy, not only because new seating obscures the original remains beneath, but also because the view to the city has been lost. Whatever your opinion, however, you cannot fail to be impressed by the building's elegance.

Perched on a ridge above the theatre, the castle and the remains of its 1 km- (1/2 mile-) long Roman and medieval walls are a spectacular sight. The bulk of what can be seen today was built as a Moorish fortress in the 11th century.

Close to the castle there is also a small archaeological museum (see page 134).

Sagunt's arcaded main square, overlooked by the church of Santa María and the town hall, was the hub of medieval life in the town. On the way from there to the castle you will pass through the

◐ *This is what the world's biggest food fight looks like*

narrow streets and pointed archways of the Jewish quarter, between neat, whitewashed houses.

Theatre & Castle ⓐ C/del Castillo ⓣ 962 66 55 81 ⓛ 10.00–20.00 Tues–Sat, 10.00–14.00 Sun & public holidays, closed Mon

BUÑOL AND *LA TOMATINA*

Some 38 km (24 miles) to the west of Valencia is the small town of Buñol. For 364 days of the year, this is a pretty and unassuming place, where the occasional visitors come to wander through the medieval streets lined with whitewashed houses. Check out the 13th-century castle and maybe strike out for a walk in the surrounding pine-covered hills.

The day that makes Buñol famous is the last Wednesday in August, when the streets are jammed with thousands of visitors for the tomato-throwing mayhem that is *La Tomatina* festival. The fiesta is thought to have started in 1945 after a fight in the town square got out of hand and the tomatoes from a nearby stall were used as missiles; everyone enjoyed it so much they went back and did it again on the same date the following year (with their own tomatoes)!

Today lorry-loads of the red fruit are brought in and once the first banger sounds at 12.00, around 30,000 people throw them, until they and the whole town are smeared in a thick layer of tomato purée. The madness of what is probably the world's biggest food fight is officially brought to an end by a second banger at 13.00. For more information about *La Tomatina*, visit ⓦ www.latomatina.es ⓣ Train: local line C3 services depart frequently from Estación del Norte in the centre of Valencia

Tourist Information ⓐ Plaza Cronista Chabret ⓣ 962 65 58 59
ⓦ www.sagunt.com ⓛ 08.00–15.00, 16.00–18.30 Mon–Fri,
09.00–12.00 Sat, Sun & public holidays

CULTURE

Museo Arqueológico, Sagunt

A small, but rewarding, archaeological museum, close to the castle,
where you will find fascinating Bronze Age artefacts alongside
various Roman mosaics and inscriptions. ⓐ C/Castillo ⓣ 962 66 55 81
ⓛ 10.00–18.00 Tues–Sat, 10.00–14.00 Sun & public holidays, closed
Mon, Nov–Mar; 10.00–20.00 Tues–Sat, 10.00–14.00 Sun & public
holidays, closed Mon, Apr–Oct. Admission charge

Roman Theatre, Sagunt

A spectacular venue is now used for open-air performances.
A good time to catch one is during the *Sagunt a Escena*
performing arts festival in July and August. ⓐ C/Teatro Romano
ⓣ 963 53 92 00 ⓦ www.teatres.gva.es

TAKING A BREAK

RESTAURANTS

El Puig

Alhacena ££ Perfect for lunch or dinner, this traditional restaurant
has a bewildering array of starters, rice dishes and fabulous
fresh fish. ⓐ Av. Virgen del Puig 36 ⓣ 961 47 13 40 ⓛ 13.30–16.00,
21.00–24.00 Tues–Sat, 13.30–16.00 Sun, closed Mon (summer);
21.00–24.00 Thur–Sat (winter)

Huerto de Santa María ££ The varied wine menu is an added bonus in this restaurant serving good traditional rice, meat and fish recipes. ⓐ Camino de Cebolla 4 ⓣ 961 47 22 26 ⓦ www.huertodesantamaria.com ⓛ 13.30–15.30 Tues–Sun, closed Mon

Sagunt

L'Armeler ££ Tucked away in the Jewish quarter in a charming old building, its dinky menu has French and Mediterranean dishes, with excellent salads. ⓐ C/Castillo 44 ⓣ 962 66 43 82 ⓦ www.larmeler.com ⓛ 13.30–16.00 Tues & Wed, 13.30–16.00, 20.45–23.00 Thur–Sat, closed Sun

Le Fou ££ Right in front of the Roman theatre, this is the perfect place to dine if you're seeing a show. A menu of creative food with a French influence. ⓐ C/Castillo 49 ⓣ 962 65 13 57 ⓛ 13.30–16.00, 21.00–23.30 Tues–Sat, 13.30–16.00 Sun & Mon

Port of Sagunt

El Jabalí Alegre £ This restaurant only opens at weekends, but has a great atmosphere and excellent value food. ⓐ C/Isla Cerdeña 29 ⓣ 618 63 57 35 ⓦ www.eljabalialegre.com ⓛ 21.00–late Fri, Sat & eves of public holidays, 14.00–late Sun & public holidays, closed Mon–Thur

Negresca ££ Mediterranean cuisine with some welcome inventive twists and friendly service, too. ⓐ Av. del Mediterráneo 141 ⓣ 962 68 04 04 ⓦ www.negresca.net ⓛ 13.00–16.00, 20.30–23.30 Tues–Sat, 13.00–16.00 Sun, closed Mon

Benicàssim

La Manduca £ Just a trot from the beach, in the centre of Benicàssim, this place offers great Italian food. Interesting wine list. ⓐ C/Santo

Tomás 69 ☎ 964 30 17 18 ⓦ www.lamanduca.net 🕐 13.00–16.00,
20.00–24.00

Restaurante La Llar £ An excellent purveyor of the region's
rice specialities, including paella, with additional daily specials.
ⓐ C/Santa Agueda 9 ☎ 964 30 55 59 🕐 13.30–15.30, 20.30–23.30
Tues–Sat, 13.30–16.30 Sun, closed Mon

ACCOMMODATION

If you wish to stop over in Sagunt, there are a few options near the
Old Town, which, although not luxurious, should be perfectly adequate
for a short stay. There are plenty more places in nearby Port de Sagunt
that have the added advantage of being close to the beach.

El Bergantín £ A simple, homely, typically Spanish hotel, with
all you need to wash off the sand and sleep off the sangria.
ⓐ Pl. del Sol, Port de Sagunt ☎ 962 68 03 59

Hotel Azahar £ Probably the best of the bunch, this modern building,
close to the train station but a short walk from the Old Town, has
basic rooms that are comfortable and clean. ⓐ Av. País Valencia 8
☎ 962 66 33 68 📠 962 65 01 75 ✉ hotelazahar@msn.com

Benicàssim also has several beachfront hotels, the best of which is:
Hotel Voramar ££ Built right on the north end of the beach, this large
hotel has great views and is ideal for festival-goers or holidaymakers.
ⓐ Paseo Pilar Coloma 1 ☎ 964 30 01 50 ⓦ www.voramar.net

● *Your first glimpse of Valencia may be of its* modernista *style*

PRACTICAL INFORMATION

Directory

GETTING THERE

By air

Valencia's Aeropuerto de Manises is increasingly well served by low-cost airlines flying from various UK and European airports. The flight time from London is approximately two hours. If you are travelling from Scotland or struggling to find a cheap ticket it is also worth considering flying to Alicante on the Costa Blanca, which is only 130km (80 miles) away. The best deals are usually reserved for those who book on-line, well in advance.

Aerlingus fly from Dublin. ☎ 0818 365 000 (Ireland), 0870 8765000 (UK) ⓦ www.aerlingus.com

British Airways fly from London Gatwick. ☎ 0870 8509 850 ⓦ www.ba.com

Easyjet fly from London Gatwick, London Stansted and Bristol. ☎ 0871 244 2366 ⓦ www.easyjet.com

Flyglobespan fly to Alicante from Edinburgh and Glasgow. ☎ 08712 710 415 ⓦ www.flyglobespan.com

Iberia fly from London Heathrow. ☎ 0870 609 0500 ⓦ www.iberia.com

Jet2 fly from Manchester, Leeds and Newcastle. ☎ 0871 226 1737 ⓦ www.jet2.com

Ryanair fly from London Stansted and Liverpool. ☎ 0871 2460000 ⓦ www.ryanair.com

Thomson fly from Bournemouth, Coventry and Doncaster Sheffield. ☎ 0870 1900 737 ⓦ www.thomsonfly.com

Many people are aware that air travel emits CO_2, which contributes to climate change. You may be interested in the possibility of lessening

● *The new terminal of Valencia's Aeropuerto de Manises*

the environmental impact of your flight through Climate Care, which offsets your CO_2 by funding environmental projects around the world. Visit Ⓦ www.climatecare.org

By rail

Such is the distance involved that rail travel from London to Valencia turns into a marathon journey of more than 30 hours. Take the Eurostar to Paris Gare du Nord, then find your way to Paris's Austerlitz station to catch the overnight train to Perpignan, from where a train will take you directly to Valencia's magnificent Estación del Norte in the city centre. This is unlikely to be a budget option, but will at least leave you free to enjoy the spectacular scenery of some of Spain's Mediterranean coast.

Eurostar Ⓣ 08705 186186 Ⓦ www.eurostar.com
Euro Railways Ⓣ 0870 584 8848 Ⓦ www.eurorailways.com

By road

Only consider driving to Spain from the UK if the road trip is intended to be part of your holiday, because it is a long way (about 1,900 km or 1,200 miles from London to Valencia). The drive through France and Spain will take two or three days and tolls are payable on the motorways of both countries.

For those with a super-human tolerance of confined spaces, coach travel is a reasonably priced option, with extra discounts for under-25s, OAPs and those with disabilities. The journey from London Victoria takes some 30 hours, including a change in Barcelona, and arrives in Valencia's Estación Central de Autobuses, which is, thankfully, just a 15-minute walk from the cafés in Barrio del Carmen.

Eurolines buses can be booked through National Express (Ⓣ 08705 808080. Ⓦ www.nationalexpress.com) in the UK.

By water

Ferries ply routes between England's south coast and the ports of
Santander and Bilbao. Although they can be expensive, these trips
might be more fun than being cooped-up in the car, but there is
still a substantial drive after the ferry crossing, of about 600 km
(375 miles) from Bilbao and 640 km (415 miles) from Santander.

Brittany Ferries sail from Plymouth to Santander. ☎ 08709 076 103
ⓦ www.brittany-ferries.co.uk

Eurotunnel will take you from Folkestone to Calais. ☎ 08705 353535
ⓦ www.eurotunnel.com

P&O Ferries sail from Portsmouth to Bilbao. ☎ 08705 980333
ⓦ www.poferries.com

Visitors from elsewhere in Europe should travel via their
nearest major city, all of which have plane and train connections
to Valencia.

Travellers from North America fly via Barcelona; travellers from
Australia and New Zealand fly via Madrid.

ENTRY FORMALITIES

Citizens of the UK, Republic of Ireland, other EU countries, the USA,
Canada, Australia and New Zealand are all permitted to enter Spain
with a valid passport. A visa is required if the duration of the stay is
more than 90 days. Visitors from South Africa need to ensure that
they have a valid passport and visa, return or onward travel tickets
and sufficient funds for their stay.

Visitors to Spain from within the EU are entitled to bring their
personal effects and goods for personal consumption and not for
resale, which can be up to 800 cigarettes and ten litres of spirits. Those
entering the country from outside the EU may bring 200 cigarettes
(50 cigars, 250g tobacco), two litres of wine or one litre of spirits.

◆ *If you are already in Spain, you can reach Valencia by rail*

No meat or dairy products are permitted to be brought into the country from inside or outside the EU.

MONEY

Spain's currency is the euro. Easily distinguishable notes are available in denominations of 5, 10, 20, 50, 100, 200 and 500 euros, while coins worth 1, 2, 5, 10, 20 and 50 cents, as well as 1 and 2 euros are widely used.

There are plenty of banks (*bancos*) and savings banks (*caixes d'estalvis/cajas de ahorros*) in the city, except in the winding streets of the historic centre. Tourist hotspots such as Plaza de la Reina and the shopping streets are well-served by banks and ATMs. The most convenient option is to obtain cash from one of the numerous ATMs, attached to the bank buildings, with your debit or credit card. Almost all ATMs in Valencia accept international cards, but your bank is likely to charge a fee for such withdrawals. All of the banks will accept traveller's cheques (with your passport), but will charge a commission. There are also bureaux de change offices in the same tourist areas as the banks and while some of them may not charge commission, their exchange rate will usually be lower.

Credit cards are generally accepted in the city's hotels, shops and restaurants, but don't assume that smaller establishments and museums will take plastic payment. If in any doubt, ask before embarrassment occurs.

HEALTH, SAFETY & CRIME

Valencia's drinking water is guaranteed as safe by the government, but many people prefer to drink bottled water, because what comes out of the tap tastes slightly unpleasant. Bear this in mind when waiters try and persuade you towards drinking bottled water in restaurants. The city's food should present no health risk to travellers.

Spain's public healthcare system is very good, and thanks to a reciprocal agreement, citizens of the UK and other EU countries are entitled to free medical treatment following the presentation of a valid European Health Insurance Card (EHIC). The EHIC is not accepted by private medical practices in Spain and does not entitle holders to free dental treatment (except emergency extractions). Apply for the EHIC on-line at Ⓦ www.dh.gov.uk/travellers and allow at least a week to receive the card. It is standard practice in Spanish hospitals to request ID from patients, so make sure that you have your passport with you.

Remember that the EHIC is no substitute for personal medical insurance and will not cover repatriation for medical treatment. Nationals of non-EU countries should ensure that they have adequate medical cover before travelling.

Tourists in Valencia are not often the victims of crime and it is a safe place to visit, but keep an eye on your valuables in busy areas, because pickpockets will always be on the lookout for an easy target.

OPENING HOURS

Banks generally open between 08.30 and 14.30 from Monday to Friday and some also open on Saturday morning. During the week shops begin trading from 09.00 or 10.00 until around 14.00, when they close for at least two hours, opening again at around 16.00 until 20.00 or 21.00. They may not open again on Saturday afternoons and very few open on Sunday. Increasingly, the larger chain and department stores are abandoning lunchtime closing.

Most museums in the city are closed on Mondays.

Despite air-conditioning, the hot months of July and August is still when many businesses close for their holidays and many of the city's residents pack up and head somewhere cooler. So if you visit at this time expect things to be a bit quiet (except at the beach).

TOILETS

Public toilets are non-existent in Valencia, so visitors to the city must rely on the facilities provided in museums, shops and cafés, which are free of charge. The many El Corte Inglés department stores on the shopping streets at the edge of the Old City are a reliable bet if other alternatives are not apparent.

CHILDREN

Few countries include children as completely as Spain. Whole families enjoy late dinners in restaurants, where the younger members are welcomed rather than tolerated and there are great playgrounds, parks and, of course, beaches where everyone can relax and enjoy the sunshine. The main supermarkets, like Consum and Mercadona, sell national and international brands of nappies, tissues, baby food, etc.

Bioparc Valencia (see page 90) is always a great place for the children to see and learn about animals from countries all over the world, while at Parque de Cabecera (Headwaters Park, see page 100) you can hire a swan-shaped pedalo for an hour and cruise around the lake (life-jackets provided for kids). Bring a picnic or just something to feed the eager ducks and goldfish. Another fabulous open-air option is the Jardines de Real Viveros (Royal Gardens, see page 94). The park here is full of playgrounds for children, plus there's a cycling circuit, bird houses and also a little train chugging around. Ciutat de les Arts i de les Cienciês (City of Arts and Sciences, see page 90) is a striking, modern complex boasting an IMAX cinema, science museum (where children are encouraged to touch exhibits) and fantastic aquarium with an entertaining dolphin show. A combined *entrada conjunta* ticket lets you spend two

⬤ *Swanning around Headwaters Park is great fun*

educational days here. Just a few minutes from the city centre, Malvarrosa Beach (see page 99) is safe for swimming and water sports (weather permitting), and the perfect place to play. It is packed in August, so supervise children closely to avoid losing them in the crowd. Turia River Park (see page 100), the beautiful park that runs across the city in the old river bed, is ideal for picnics, football and frisbee. It has plenty of playgrounds along its length, but the best is Gulliver, where a giant lies on the ground, covered in ramps and slides; here, children can play at being Lilliputians.

COMMUNICATIONS
Internet
There are internet cafés around the city, particularly close to the university, but most hotels offer access, too.

ONO.COM This is an immense broadband internet centre, with 130 computers, webcams, scanners, fax machines, etc., right in the middle of town, near Plaza del Ayuntamiento.

ⓐ C/San Vicente Mártir 22 ① 963 28 19 02 Ⓦ www.ono.com
Ⓛ 09.00–22.00 Mon–Fri, 10.00–22.00 Sat & Sun
Ⓝ Metro: Xátiva, Plaza España; bus: 7, 27, 81

Phone
If you need to make a phone call in Valencia, you will not have to go far before you find a public phone booth. Most of these will give operating instructions in English at the touch of a button and accept euro coins and phonecards, which can be purchased from tobacconists. To make a call, lift the receiver, insert a coin and wait for a dial tone before proceeding. Many bars, hotels and restaurants also have phones for public use.

TELEPHONING SPAIN

To phone from abroad, dial your international access code, then the national code for Spain, 34. The area code for Valencia is 96, but this still needs to be dialled from within the city.

TELEPHONING ABROAD

To phone home from Valencia dial the outgoing code 00, followed by the relevant country code: UK 44, Rep of Ireland 353, USA and Canada 1, Australia 61, New Zealand 64, South Africa 27.

International calls are cheaper after 22.00 on weekdays, 14.00 on Saturdays and all day Sunday. Local telephone offices (*locutorios*), where you can call from private booths, often offer the best rates for international calls.

If you plan to use your mobile phone abroad, check with your service provider that you will be able to access the relevant networks.

Post

Spain has an efficient postal service (*Correos*) and its sunny yellow offices and post boxes are easy to spot. Stamps can be purchased at post offices or from tobacconists. It costs €0.58 to send a postcard to Europe and €0.78 to the rest of the world. The central post office is at Plaza de Ayuntamiento 24.

ELECTRICITY

The electricity supply in Valencia is at 220–240V AC 50Hz and the socket design means that adapters are required for UK electrical appliances, while those from the USA will need a transformer as well.

TRAVELLERS WITH DISABILITIES

Valencia is an ancient city and many of its buildings, beaches and narrow winding streets were not designed for those with disabilities. However, the Town Hall has been investing heavily in access in the last few years and huge improvements have been made.

Almost all buses now have lowering steps and ramps and almost all metro stations are also fully accessible. The new Bailén Intermodal train station has been specially designed with the needs of visually impaired travellers in mind. Ramps and improvements in paving mean that most areas of the city are fairly accessible and many museums have made adaptations to accommodate disabled visitors. Don't be afraid to ask for help if needed.

Major beaches around Valencia have ramps and walkways to reach the sea, and in some areas it is possible to hire an aquatic wheelchair. The tourist information office can help with lists of accessible hotels in the city and surrounding area, but you should always call the hotel directly and be clear about your needs.

The best source of information is the main tourism information website Ⓦ www.turisvalencia.es. Click on 'Accessible Valencia' or the wheelchair icon for a full English-language description of facilities and contacts. The **Disabled Persons Transport Advisory Committee** (Ⓦ www.dptac.gov.uk/door-to-door) gives some useful advice on flying to foreign destinations.

TOURIST INFORMATION

The English-speaking staff at the offices of Valencia Tourism are a useful source of maps, accommodation and events information. There are branches at:

Old City

(a) Pl. de la Reina 19 (t) 963 15 39 31 (w) www.turisvalencia.es
(b) 09.00–19.00 Mon–Sat, 10.00–14.00 Sun & holidays
(m) Metro: Colón, Plaza España; bus: 4, 6, 8, 9, 11
(a) C/Poeta Querol (next to the Main Theatre) (t) 963 51 49 07
(w) www.valenciaterraimar.com (b) 9.30–19.00 Mon–Fri, 10.00–14.00
Sat, 11.00–14.00 Sun (m) Metro: Colón; bus: 36, 16, 10, 8, 6
(a) C/Paz 48 (t) 963 98 64 22 (w) www.comunitatvalenciana.com
(e) valencia@touristinfo.net (b) 09.00–20.00 Mon–Fri,
10.00–20.00 Sat, 10.00–14.00 Sun (m) Metro: Colón; bus: 6, 8, 9, 11, 16

🔽 The bus and metro network make it easy to explore the city

Beach

ⓐ Paseo de Neptuno 2 (opposite Hotel Neptuno) ⓣ 963 55 71 08
Ⓦ www.turisvalencia.es ⓛ 10.00–19.00 Mon–Fri, 10.00–18.00 Sat,
Sun & public holidays Ⓜ Metro: Neptú; bus: 32

Rail station

ⓐ C/Xátiva 24 (Estación del Norte) ⓣ 963 52 85 73
Ⓦ www.turisvalencia.es ⓛ 09.00–19.00 Mon–Sat, 10.00–14.00 Sun
& holidays Ⓜ Metro: Xátiva; bus: 5, 19, 35

Airport

ⓐ Arrivals hall ⓣ 961 53 02 29 Ⓦ www.turisvalencia.com
ⓛ 08.30–20.30 Mon–Fri, 09.30–17.30 Sat, Sun & holidays
Ⓜ Metro: Aeroport

Two official tourism websites offer all the information you could
need in English about the city and its history, events and facilities:
Valencia Tourism Ⓦ www.turisvalencia.es
Valencia Council Ⓦ www.valencia.es

BACKGROUND READING

Reeds and Mud by Vicente Blasco Ibañéz (translated by
Cañas y Barro). The author depicts the hardships of village
life near the Albufera lake and centres on the conflict between
generations of fishermen and the consequences of a forbidden
love affair.
Travelers' Tales: Spain, edited by Lucy McCauly. This compendium
contains an excellent essay by Louis de Bernières about *La Tomatina*.

Emergencies

The number to call for any kind of emergency is ❶ 112. Apart from that, the fire service and each police force have its own dedicated number. If in doubt, dial 112 to speak to a multilingual operator. If there is a medical emergency while you are at your hotel, the reception staff should be able to call an ambulance for you.

Fire ❶ 080
Policía Local ❶ 092
Policía Nacional ❶ 091
Lost property ❶ 963 52 54 78 (only Mon–Fri)

MEDICAL SERVICES

Doctors & dentists

Lists of local doctors and dentists can be found in telephone directories and may also be obtained by contacting the relevant consulate, which will have information on English-speaking practitioners. In a sudden emergency your hotel should be able to summon a doctor for you.

Hospitals

There are a number of public hospitals in Valencia, which will treat tourists holding a European Health Insurance Card (EHIC) without charge in an emergency. Make sure that any hospital that you attend is not privately run, otherwise you will be asked to pay for your treatment in full.

EMERGENCY PHRASES

Help!	**Fire!**	**Stop!**
¡Socorro!	¡Fuego!	¡Stop!
¡Sawkoro!	*¡Fwegoh!*	*¡Stop!*

Call an ambulance/a doctor/the police/the fire service!
¡Llame a una ambulancia/un médico/la policía/a los bomberos!
*¡Lliame a oona anboolanthea/oon meydico/la poletheea/
a lohs bombehrohs!*

The following hospitals have emergency departments:
Hospital General Universitario de Valencia ⓐ Av. de las Tres Cruces
ⓣ 963 86 27 00
Hospital Ciudad Sanitaria la Fe ⓐ Av. Campanar 21 ⓣ 963 86 27 00

POLICE

There are two police forces; the *Policía Local* deal with minor
matters, such as traffic offences, and wear a blue-and-yellow
uniform, while the blue-uniformed *Policía Nacional* deal with
weightier problems like drugs and terrorism.

City-centre police stations are open 24 hours a day and should
be contacted by their own individual telephone numbers when
the situation is not an emergency.

Cases of theft should be reported to the local police at the
earliest opportunity so that any relevant documentation for
an insurance claim can be completed.

Policía Local  Av. del Cid 37 963 840 092 24-hours
Metro: Avda del Cid
Policía Nacional Gran Vía Ramón y Cajal 963 539 539
24-hours Metro: Angel Guimerá

EMBASSIES & CONSULATES

The closest British Consulate is located in Barcelona. Staff there can assist British nationals in emergencies by: arranging for next of kin to be informed of death or hospitalisation; giving advice on obtaining emergency funds from friends or relatives; issuing emergency passports; contacting British nationals in prison on request. However, the consulate cannot get British nationals out of prison, give legal advice or pay outstanding bills.

Australian Pl. Gala Placidia 1, Barcelona 934 90 09 13
British Torre de Barcelona Av. Diagonal 477-13º, Barcelona
933 66 62 00
Canadian Nunez de Balboa 35, Madrid 914 23 32 50
Irish Torre Oeste, Gran Vía Carlos III, 94, Barcelona
934 91 50 21
United States C/Paz 6, Valencia 963 51 69 73
New Zealand Travesera de Gracia 64, Barcelona 932 09 0399
South African Las Mercedes 31–4, Bilbao 944 80 03 28

Valencia is a great destination to explore

INDEX

WHAT'S IN YOUR GUIDEBOOK?

Independent authors Impartial up-to-date information from our travel experts who meticulously source local knowledge.

Experience Thomas Cook's 165 years in the travel industry and guidebook publishing enriches every word with expertise you can trust.

Travel know-how Contributions by thousands of staff around the globe, each one living and breathing travel.

Editors Travel-publishing professionals, pulling everything together to craft a perfect blend of words, pictures, maps and design.

You, the traveller We deliver a practical, no-nonsense approach to information, geared to how you really use it.

ACKNOWLEDGEMENTS & FEEDBACK

Editorial/project management: Lisa Plumridge with Laetitia Clapton
Copy editor: Paul Hines
Layout/DTP: Alison Rayner
Proofreader: Wendy Janes

The publishers would like to thank the following individuals and organisations for supplying their copyright photographs for this book: A1 Pix, pages 5, 9, 21, 101, 132 & 142; Hannu Liivaar/Dreamstime.com, page 47; Hans Geel/Dreamstime.com, page 48; Iberimages, pages 120–1, 129 & 130; Inbocca, page 110; La Casa Azul, page 35; Renee Miguel Sara Querecuto van der Muelen, page 139; Fernando Sanchez/iStockphoto.com, page 65; Roberto A Sanchez/iStockphoto.com, page 25; Turismo Valencia, pages 7, 13, 17, 26–7, 28, 57, 75, 76–7, 98 & 137; Carlos Vernich/iStockphoto.com, page 61; Lee Walton/Fotolia, page 62; Malcolm Dodds, all others.

Send your thoughts to
books@thomascook.com

- **Found a great bar, club, shop or must-see sight that we don't feature?**
- **Like to tip us off about any information that needs a little updating?**
- **Want to tell us what you love about this handy little guidebook and more importantly how we can make it even handier?**

Then here's your chance to tell all! Send us ideas, discoveries and recommendations today and then look out for your valuable input in the next edition of this title.

Email the above address (stating the title) or write to: CitySpots Project Editor, Thomas Cook Publishing, PO Box 227, Coningsby Road, Peterborough PE3 8SB, UK.